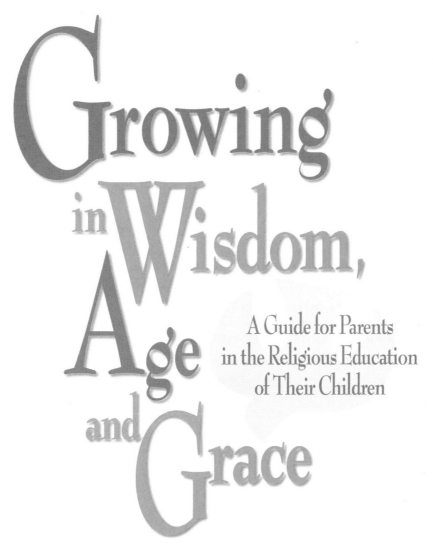

Growing in Wisdom, Age and Grace

A Guide for Parents
in the Religious Education
of Their Children

Joseph Cardinal Bernardin

REVISED EDITION

William H. Sadlier , Inc.
9 Pine Street
New York, New York 10005-1002

ACKNOWLEDGMENTS

Sister Anne Leonard, CND; when she was Director of the Department of Educational Services in the Archdiocese of Chicago, commissioned a Task Force to research and design this parent guide. Father John Pollard, formerly Director of Religious Education for the Archdiocese of Chicago, managed the Task Force which was composed of parents, parish directors of religious education, principals, teachers, catechists and professional consultants. I am deeply grateful to Sister Anne Leonard, CND, Father John Pollard and the Task Force members for their invaluable assistance in the preparation of this parent guide.

Rev. John Pollard, Chairman
Sr. Peg Barrett, RSM
Mrs. Patricia DiNaso
Sr. Ellenine Goldthwaite, BVM
Ms. Joan Hilby
Mrs. Katherine Jackson
Mrs. Elizabeth McMahon Jeep

Mrs. Jean Noble
Sr. Mary Kay O'Brien, BVM
Mr. John Price
Mrs. Haydee Ruiz
Mrs. Elizabeth Villanueva
Sr. Felicia Wolf, OSF

In addition, I want to thank those many parents and professional religious educators who contributed their insights and experiences to the refinement of the manuscript. I particularly wish to acknowledge:

Dr. Carole Eipers, Director of Religious Education
Mrs. Sue Bordenaro, Consultant, Office for Religious Education
Rev. Alphonse Spilly, Special Assistant to Cardinal

Joseph Cardinal Bernardin

Contents

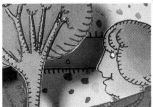

A Letter to Parents

Dear Parents,

The call to be a Catholic parent—to nurture the faith in your child and to share it in your family—makes you the first herald of the gospel for your child. Through the witness of lives informed by active, conscious faith, parents respond to that call in a manner which enriches them and their children. A parent walks with a child under the guidance of the Holy Spirit, who directs the growth of each "in wisdom and age and grace."

At times, I know, being a parent can seem an overwhelming and lonely task. You sometimes feel that society does not support your efforts, that television and other media demean your family values, or even that the Church has left you on your own to struggle with the questions you face in raising your children as Catholics.

This guide is intended to affirm and assist you in your efforts to share your faith with your children. It is meant to be both an appealing invitation and a gentle challenge. Inviting you to view yourself as God's partner in the creation of a domestic church—the family—it also challenges you to view your family as a community of persons who encounter the Lord in and with one another.

What is said here is not intended to paint a rosy picture of family life or to make you feel inadequate as a parent. There is no ideal family. There are no perfect parents. There is no single, "correct" way to nurture children. Family composition, cultural tradition, economic background, and other factors make each family unique. There are many ways to build strong Catholic families, and many qualities which are distinctively Catholic. Some of those methods and traits are discussed here.

This guide is divided into six sections. The first describes family life today. The next five correspond to the stages in the development of children: infants, young children, primary grade children, intermediate grade children, and young adolescents. In each section, three interrelated aspects of development are treated: family life, prayer life, and Church life. However, it is important to bear in mind that children do not develop at the same pace, and the stages of development frequently overlap.

Perhaps the most fundamental contribution you can make to the religious formation of your children is to mature in faith yourself. This guide is therefore concerned with the development of your faith, not only because you are a parent, but because you are a child of God. Intended for you, it is also dedicated to you. Yours is a great and beautiful vocation: to nurture a new generation of loving, informed, and committed followers of Jesus. I pray that what follows may help you fulfill that admirable trust.

Asking God's blessings on you and your family, I am

Devotedly yours in Christ,

Joseph Cardinal Bernardin

Joseph Cardinal Bernardin

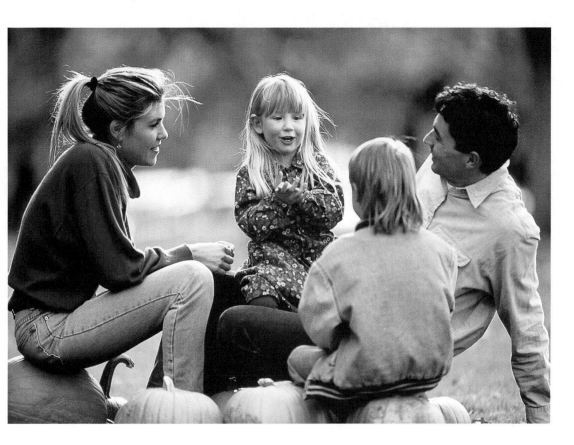

Today's
Family

THE PARENT

A parent instinctively shares those beliefs that he or she holds most deeply. Parents are therefore more capable of sharing their faith than they may realize. Faith adds an extra dimension to parental love, transforming everyday encounters into occasions when faith is spoken, celebrated, and lived. While nurturing human values, such as security and trust, the parent at the same time lays the foundation for religious values, such as the love of God and dependence on God's care. "The family is the community in which, from childhood, one can learn moral values, begin to honor God, and make good use of freedom" (*Catechism of the Catholic Church*, 2207). For parents, God's affirming and forgiving love provides the model for their love of their children. For children, parental love is a concrete sign of God's love.

Parents do not wait until children begin school to teach them to speak or to walk, nor do they wait until then to teach children that God is good and loving. Formal programs of religious formation are important helps, yet they can only supplement the child's experience of living in a Christian home. Programs cannot replace parents in the religious formation of children.

From the moment of conception, a child depends primarily on the parent. As a parent provides nourishment, warmth, rest, and security for a child, he or she also encourages the life of faith. From the beginning, it is more important for a parent to spend time with a child than to spend money on a child.

A parent influences the religious development of a child initially and powerfully. A parent is the fundamental model and first teacher of faith for a child. A parent shares faith with a child by speaking of faith and by good example. Simply by living in the family a child observes and begins to imitate the parent's beliefs and values. Children will have many teachers, but their parents are unique.

The family is the community in which, from childhood, one can learn moral values, begin to honor God, and make good use of freedom.

Catechism of the Catholic Church, 2207

CHANGES IN THE FAMILY

Family life has changed in the last several decades. People move more often. The "traditional" family, in which the father works outside the home and the mother keeps house and raises the children, is more and more uncommon today. Often both parents work, in some situations because of economic necessity, but in other cases because of women's desires to enhance their personal growth, meet financial responsibilities, and contribute their gifts. Unemployment has also become a serious threat to family life. Thus, finding new ways to maintain family "closeness" has become a formidable challenge. "It is necessary to go back to seeing the family as the sanctuary of life" (*Encyclical on the 100th Anniversary of "Rerum Novarum,"* 39).

Since mothers often work outside the home, fathers have become more active in raising children. Many women have developed themselves in ways that before were unavailable to them. At the same time, many men are enriched by their involvement in nurturing their children.

SINGLE PARENTS

Single parents head a growing number of Catholic families. Often a parent raising children alone bears complete responsibility for the welfare of the family and must work outside the home. This absence may trouble the single parent. Struggling to fill so many roles, overburdened by responsibilities, he or she may not take time to attend to personal or social needs.

Many single parents find joy and satisfaction in raising their children and seeing them begin to live successfully on their own. Sometimes a single parent's own parents or other family members become more involved and the family bonds among them grow stronger.

Single parents face special difficulties, but they share the fundamental challenge facing all parents. No parent can meet all the needs of his or her child.

And even though one parent cannot be two parents, a single parent can take special care to bring his or her child into contact with both feminine and masculine models of Christian living.

Sharing their experiences with other parents and families can often help single parents feel more secure. They might benefit from helping to organize support groups or special gatherings for parents and families in their parishes. A single parent may offer to watch another single parent's children for a few hours one day in exchange for the same favor on another day. Single parents need to speak up in parishes to ensure that educational, liturgical, and service programs are sensitive to their needs.

DIVORCE

In a culture in which divorce and remarriage are widely accepted, married couples face serious challenges in living out their permanent, faithful, and life-giving commitment. The Church's pastoral concern extends in a special way to those who experience divorce. They rightfully look to the Catholic community to provide a support system that expresses this concern. Divorced persons and their children should be welcomed by every parish community and encouraged to participate fully in parish life.

Some divorced persons will ask the Church to investigate the validity of their marriages and will seek a declaration of nullity. If an annulment is granted, they may marry again, in which case a new family comes into being and new relationships among parents and children are formed.

This situation involves opportunities and challenges of its own. Feelings of guilt, lowered self-esteem, hurt, and bewilderment may be present in parents who have recently experienced divorce and in their children. New relationships within blended families are not always easily established. Doing so can be a valuable experience for parents and children, although the issues that arise are frequently perplexing and not quickly resolved.

INTERFAITH MARRIAGE AND FAMILY LIFE

The number of interreligious marriages continues to grow. Such marriages raise special questions for the religious development of children. While religious traditions often have similar beliefs, differences should have been discussed openly and honestly before the couple marry and continue to be part of an ongoing dialogue during the marriage. In this way, each partner's respective tradition can have an appropriate place in the family. As in every marriage, good communication between husband and wife in a religiously "mixed" marriage smoothes most difficulties.

In the period of preparation before an interfaith marriage, the Catholic partner reaffirms his or her Catholic faith and promises to share it with the children of the marriage by doing all in their power to have them baptized and raised as Catholics. Even so, the religious formation of the children will involve sensitive decisions, best made by both partners together. In an interdenominational or interfaith family, as in any other, it is not the particular differences or similarities in beliefs or practices but the good example of family members and their mutual love that most deeply affect the religious development of children.

VARIETY IN FAMILY STRUCTURES

The family is where everyone should be confident of being loved and accepted. Married couples living together with their children, older couples with children who have left home, childless couples, single parents and their children, families created by adoption, migrant and immigrant families, separated couples with children—these are all families. God loves them all. So should all of us.

GRANDPARENTS AND OTHERS WHO CARE FOR CHILDREN

Grandparents, aunts, uncles, and extended family members are often involved in the religious formation of children. They comprise a large circle of affirmation and support for children. They also challenge children to conform to family expectations. "The relationships within the family bring an affinity of feelings, affections and interests, arising above all from the members' respect for one another" (*Catechism*, 2206).

Grandparents are living proof that a family has roots, a history, a tradition. They tell children the family's story, sharing its customs and explaining its traditions.

The relationships within the family bring an affinity of feelings, affections and interests, arising above all from the members' respect for one another.

Catechism of the Catholic Church, 2206

They delight children by recalling the "old days." Often young children and their grandparents intuitively share a sense of wonder about life's simple beauty and inherent values. Although their experiences of life are very different, they often develop a unique intimacy that fosters religious development.

CHILD CARE

The number of children who receive care outside their homes is growing. Many parents' work and other activities take them away from their young ones for varying amounts of time each day. Economic pressures leave some parents with no choice in the matter.

As many are aware, parents need to be cautious in choosing the person or persons who will care for their children and conscientious in supervising those caregivers. Child care offered by others should correspond as much as possible to the parents' own approach to raising children. As extensions of the parents, caregivers should support the parents' philosophy of nurturing children. Although child care is never a substitute for the natural parent-child relationship, a proper child care environment nevertheless can supply at least some opportunity for a parent to function outside the family and also foster a sense of security and trust.

RACIAL, ETHNIC, AND CULTURAL RICHNESS OF FAMILIES

Differences among families arise from race and ethnicity, socioeconomic factors, and a multitude of other causes. Attempts to remake families according to one uniform standard, or to homogenize children's religious formation as if there were only one acceptable model, disregard the genuine religious traditions of many groups.

Distinctive cultural, racial, and ethnic characteristics, customs, and needs make family living distinctive in each tradition. Often they have a bearing on the transmission of religious values. A celebration of the birthday of Martin Luther King, Jr., a Quinceañera, Kwanzaa, a St. Patrick's Day Parade, a Mardi Gras, or a St. Joseph's Table—these are cherished practices for many people, which hand on part of their religious tradition. Parish and family celebrations of this sort link children to their religious, cultural, and ethnic history, provide them with a sense of identity and belonging, and shape strongly held values. So, for example, children who help prepare a Thanksgiving basket of food for the hungry participate in a powerful cultural tradition and also in the living out of important religious values.

PARENTS AND TEACHERS TOGETHER

Parents can also work with teachers or catechists to choose educational materials that employ language and idioms, thought patterns, customs, and symbols that respect their cultural, racial, and ethnic traditions. Thus formal education reinforces the formation taking place at home.

CHILDREN WITH SPECIAL NEEDS

Children with special needs have a special place in their families and in society. Those born with serious physical problems or mental disability, or who develop emotional or behavioral disturbances, can evoke an added measure of parental love. But they can also present difficult challenges for their parents.

Like all children, those with special needs can come to understand that God loves them unconditionally and does not ask of them what they are not capable of doing. A parent who genuinely accepts and loves such a child communicates to the child that

The family should live in such a way that its members learn to care and take responsibility for the young, the old, the sick, the handicapped, and the poor.

Catechism of the Catholic Church, 2208

he or she is worthy of God's love, as well as the love of the parent and of others. Such children provide the opportunity for learning to care for others. "The family should live in such a way that its members learn to care and take responsibility for the young, the old, the sick, the handicapped, and the poor" (*Catechism*, 2208). Still, such children require help in coming to terms with their limitations, as well as support and encouragement in all areas where growth and progress are possible. Although in many communities excellent services—including catechetical and faith formation programs—are available to children with special needs and their parents, parents of such children do sometimes encounter obstacles in securing appropriate care for them. This can place demands on their patience in a way not experienced by other parents.

A parent of a child with special needs can draw a great deal of support from meeting with others who share similar experiences. Through interaction with the wider community, such parents help the community understand the injustice of labeling and stereotyping children who have special needs.

In order to encourage the participation of developmentally disabled or brain damaged persons in their parishes and, in particular, in the worshiping community, the Archdiocese of Chicago issued a pastoral letter, "Access to the Sacraments of Initiation and Reconciliation for Developmentally Disabled Persons." While challenging the parish to provide genuine participation in sacramental preparation for the family of the developmentally disabled person, the letter also challenges the family of such a person to a deeper involvement in the religious formation of its disabled member.

HURTING FAMILIES

When problems occur, they have a way of dominating family life. From time to time, all families experience pressures, difficulties, and crises. The temporary illness of a child, for example, may disrupt your family's habit of prayer in the home or prevent you from participating in sacramental preparation meetings at the parish. But many families today face more serious problems requiring them to cope with intense, confusing emotions, such as fear, anger, inadequacy, insecurity, guilt, shame, and hurt.

Chronic illness, HIV/AIDS, alcoholism, and drug abuse often create painful family tensions. A family member's long or frequently recurring sickness can drain one's trust in God's abiding love and make it difficult for the family to celebrate the Sunday Eucharist. "Families of HIV patients badly need to talk about what they are experiencing. Although family members usually are ambivalent about disclosing the nature of their relative's disease to outsiders, it is important for them to communicate. The Catholic community should create networks of people prepared to assist such families in this way" (*Called to Compassion and Responsibility: A Response to the HIV/AIDS Crisis*, 6).

An alcoholic or drug abuser's unpredictable behavior and absence from the home can often cause strain in family relationships or their total neglect. In such situations, the family is likely to be preoccupied with health and safety. Sharing religious values can then seem rather remote from the family's immediate problems. "The family must remain the best resource for prevention, early detection, recovery, and treatment of chemical abuse. Families need to be helped to become aware of the early signs of substance abuse and those effective techniques for intervention designed to help individuals suffering from abuse to get into proper treatment or otherwise begin recovery. The family must also be involved in the treatment process and, certainly, in effective follow-up after formal treatment is completed and the recovering alcoholic or addict returns to the community" (*New Slavery, New Freedom: A Pastoral Message on Substance Abuse*, p. 9).

Separating, divorcing, and starting over can also cause families a great deal of anxiety. The natural stresses are often complicated and made worse by the legal process. Arguments centering on blame and guilt, distribution of property, and custody of children are among the distressing experiences that families often must endure even as they seek to reconstruct their lives. No wonder that families involved in such stressful changes may find it hard to praise and thank God for the wonder of creation.

Poverty, hunger, unemployment, inadequate housing, lack of educational opportunities, and many other related problems can overwhelm families struggling to provide food, shelter, safety, and security. Concentrating on these basic needs, they may find it next to impossible to tend to religious development. Although family members and caring friends may be very supportive, the situation may call for assistance from public agencies.

"Where families cannot fulfill their responsibilities, other social bodies have the duty of helping them..." (*Catechism*, 2209). Women and children in particular are frequently the victims of this endless circle of helplessness and hopelessness.

God is no stranger to hurting families. God reaches out through the family of the Church to the human community and directly to each person to transmit a healing touch. There is hope for a family's growth in faith not merely despite its overwhelming pain but, many times, precisely because of that pain.

Families need, first of all, to recognize that whatever the problem—a deteriorating marriage, an unwanted teen pregnancy, an unemployed breadwinner—it will not simply go away. Next, they need to make their pain available for healing. This involves identifying the problem, talking about it openly, and acknowledging it as theirs, and then perhaps seeking help from books and persons who can explore possible solutions with them.

This is especially true in the very serious case of child abuse within families. Experience indicates that very often the sex abuser is in a position of authority over a child, is someone the child loves and trusts. "When the person who abuses them sexually is also their parent or another trusted adult, children may find it difficulty to imagine, much less develop, a relationship with a loving God. This difficulty may be intensified if the abuser is perceived as active in the Church" (*Walk in the Light: A Pastoral Response to Child Sexual Abuse*).

The degree of harm experienced by a child can have far-reaching and long-term effects, such as guilt, withdrawal, isolation, poor self-image, inability to trust in relationships, inappropriate

Where families cannot fulfill their responsibilities, other social bodies have the duty of helping them....

Catechism of the Catholic Church, 2209

sexual behavior, inability to relate sexually with one's spouse, substance abuse, depression. Unless the cycle of abuse is broken, all too often it may continue in succeeding generations.

This is a problem that needs to be brought to light in order for healing to occur. People who have been victims of abuse need to be able to talk about their experience in order to be released from shame and guilt. Abusers need to experience forgiveness, even while they are being held accountable. The parish can be a vital means of support, by offering prayer and healing services, where people can find healing and reconciliation, by offering help and support for abusers, by developing age-appropriate programs to teach children and adults about sexual abuse issues, and by making people aware of resources and services.

In addition, family problems need to be laid reverently before God in prayer. Families need to reflect together on the place they let God occupy in their lives. They need to be open to God's healing presence. Instead of making family prayer more difficult, a problem sometimes can be an occasion for the family to express its unity with the suffering Jesus and its dependence upon the God who saves. The sacraments of Reconciliation or the Anointing of the Sick are opportunities for a family to sense the Church's healing involvement in their pain.

Reflection QUESTIONS

1. *What major changes has my extended family experienced in the past ten years?*

2. *What are the greatest joys in my family's life?*

3. *How is my family hurting right now?*

4. *How can these occasions of joy, hurt, and change be opportunities for the development of my family's faith?*

Quotations

DOCU

The Christian family constitutes a specific revelation and realization of ecclesial communion, and for this reason too it can and should be called the *domestic church*.

Pope John Paul II, On the Family, 21

As a *nation*, we need to make children and families our first priority; to invest in their future; to combat the forces—cultural, economic, and moral—which hurt children and destroy families; to manage our economy, shape our government, and direct our institutions to support and not undermine our families.

Putting Children and Families First

In God's plan the family is in many ways the first school of how to be human.

Pope John Paul II, Letter to Families, 15

The family finds in the plan of God the creator and redeemer not only its identity, what it is, but also its mission, what it can and should do. The role that God calls the family to perform in history derives from what the family is....

Pope John Paul II, On the Family, 17

Experiences teaches that human love, which naturally tends toward fatherhood and motherhood, is sometimes affected by a profound crisis and is thus seriously threatened. In such cases help can be sought at marriage and family counseling centers where it is possible, among other things, to obtain the assistance of specifically trained psychologists and psychotherapists.

Pope John Paul II, Letter to Families, 7

The families of the handicapped need care and concern, including assistance directed to helping them participate with competence and confidence in the catechesis of their handicapped members.

National Catechetical Directory, 231

from Church
MENTS

Wherever a family exists and love still moves through its members, grace is present. Nothing—not even divorce or death—can place limits on God's gracious love.
Follow the Way of Love

I want your parents, brothers and sisters, and friends to know that you are full members of the Church. By Baptism and Confirmation, you have a place in the Church that no one can ever take away from you...I want you to know that you have a place at the table of the Lord.

"Access to the Sacraments of Initiation and Reconciliation for Developmentally Disabled Persons,"
Joseph Cardinal Bernardin, Introductory Letter to the Developmentally Disabled

But remember, a family is holy not because it is perfect but because God's grace is at work in it, helping it to set out anew everyday on the way of love.
Follow the Way of Love

Families need workplace policies that promote responsive childcare arrangements; flexible employment terms and conditions for parents; and family and medical leave for parents of newborns, sick children, and aging parents.
Putting Children and Families First

The efforts of single mothers and fathers to plan and organize complicated home and work schedules and to provide the parental formation children need are inspiring. To encourage them, we recommend the formation of more single parent support groups within parishes and support for the establishment of day-care centers near homes or places of employment.
One in Christ Jesus, 71

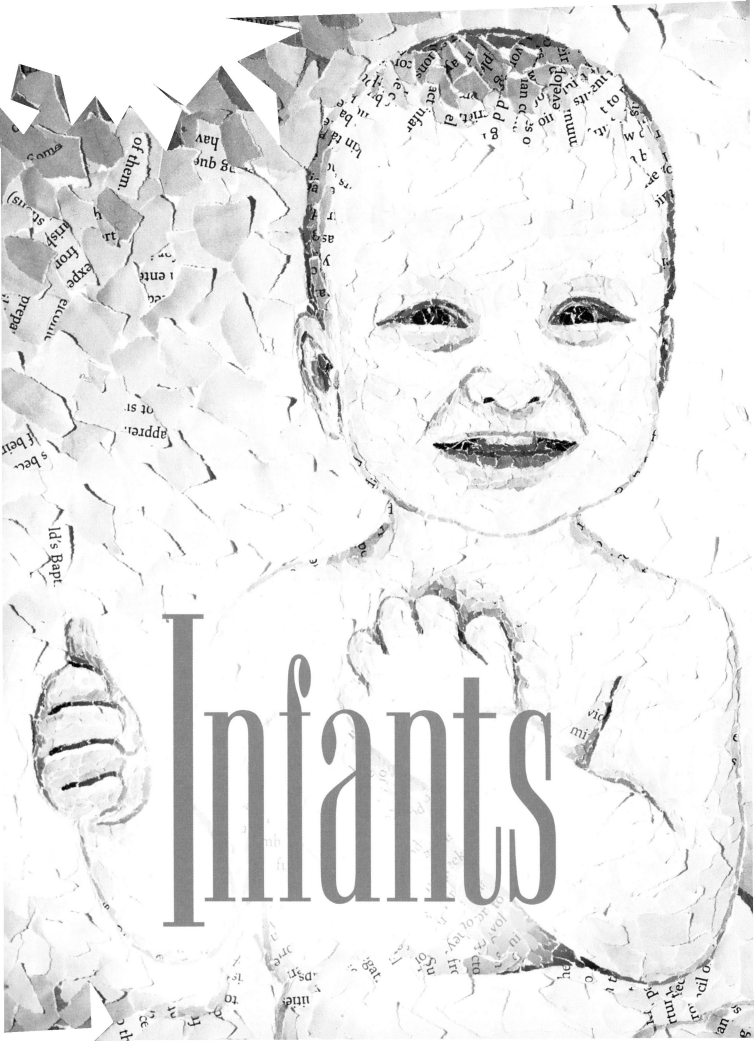

Infants

FAMILY LIFE

Sharing the gift of life is a generous and loving act. An atmosphere of unselfish love in a Christian home sets the tone for the later religious development of children. When family members help one another grow in faith by the simple witness of their Christian lives, they are already providing education in the faith.

FIRST MOMENTS OF LIFE

A family begins its relationship with an infant even during the pregnancy. Planning for the arrival of a new baby can be a project which involves all the family members. Feeling life growing inside, preparing the home, discussing the baby's impact on older children, making physical and psychological room for the baby, and sharing the news with friends are signs that a loving bond is being formed between the baby and the family.

The birth of a child is a major event in the life of every family, for a child is a most precious gift of God. Every child represents not only the loving relationship of parents, but also the loving presence of God within the family. Every parent becomes a co-creator with God of the gift of life itself.

Naming a baby can bring the values of the family into focus, inasmuch as it designates the child's specific identity within the family. The religious significance of the name, how the name sounds when spoken, and the other persons with whom the child might share the name are all important matters to consider.

The essentials of parenting, such as understanding the emotional needs of children, setting reasonable limits and establishing good health habits do not come automatically. As they relate to their infants, first-time parents will begin to realize that they need help in learning how to parent and how to adjust to changes in their other relationships. They may find study groups, meetings, or classes helpful. Conversations with other new parents, experienced and trusted family, or extended family, and with specialists in early childhood development can bring encouragement, support and peace of mind.

EARLY CHALLENGES FOR PARENTS

Parents are not perfect. Decisions about child care are frequently difficult, and often the advice is conflicting. It is normal for parents to feel confusion and self-doubt. Fatigue and lack of other adult company can also be trying for a parent of a newborn infant.

A baby's schedule is demanding. Parents of newborns, like parents in general, need to take good care of themselves, both physically and emotionally, for their own sake and the sake of their children. Plenty of rest, good companionship and a sense of humor help them cope with their weariness and frustration. Eventually, babies do grow up.

Parents have the mission of teaching their children to pray and to discover their vocation as children of God.

Catechism of the Catholic Church, 2226

EXTENDED FAMILY

Other family members and friends may form a larger circle of excitement and encouragement around a newborn child. In many families, children are raised by other caring adults in addition to a parent. Grandparents often lend a special kind of support to their children, now parents themselves. Sharing baby furniture and clothes can bring the extended family closer together and give others besides parents a sense of involvement in the baby's welfare.

THE INFANT'S WORLD

For the infant, feeling, hearing, seeing, smelling, and tasting are all that matter. Personal needs and the present moment are what count. From the infant's perspective, others exist solely to respond to his or her needs. The infant instinctively acts as if the crib were the center of the world. This is necessary and normal at the beginning of life.

The physical needs of the baby also tend to dominate the parent's life. The baby needs to be held, cuddled,

fed, changed, rocked, rubbed, covered, bathed, smiled at, talked to, sung to, and put to sleep. Eye contact and physical touch convey the parent's love and approval. And it is here, in a parent's affirming attention in the very earliest days and weeks of life, that a child's faith begins to develop.

The baby needs to be nurtured in a calm, predictable, and secure environment. Loving parental care imparts a sense of security which helps the infant respond with trust. A trusting infant-parent relationship lays the foundation for the child's positive self-image. The infant who experiences consistent parental love and attention gradually learns to trust others. For the child, the image of a loving and trustworthy God develops from within this beautiful human relationship.

PRAYER LIFE

By its nature, family life is sacred. Family prayer expresses the naturally sacred character of family life.

DAILY PRAYER

The habit of daily prayer at regular times is an important part of our religious heritage. Daily prayer is the ordinary custom of the Christian. "Parents have the mission of teaching their children to pray and to discover their vocation as children of God" (*Catechism*, 2226). Prayer with meals, in the morning, at noon, in the evening, and at the bedside marks the movement of the day and signals the wonder of God's presence throughout it.

Daily prayer in the home requires a firm commitment to make time, find a place, and be consistent.

Ideally a parent welcomes an infant into a home where daily prayer is valued. The ordinary experiences of everyday life naturally lead a parent to pause and marvel at the wonder of God's presence. The actual birth of the child, baptismal preparation, the infant's first smile, first words, first steps, first birthday, and the first anniversary of Baptism can lead a parent to praise and thank God in prayer. The natural simplicity—the elemental character—of actions like feeding, bathing, and holding an infant somehow make manifest the sacredness that abides in all loving, human interaction.

A parent usually wants a child to have a relationship with God and to express that relationship in prayer. Where a prayerful environment already exists in the home, it can be adapted to include a child just as other family routines are modified to make room for a new baby. While a parent may at first feel uncomfortable praying aloud, a modest beginning, such as pausing to ask God's protection for the new baby, can ease the hesitancy. As time goes by, a parent could softly whisper the words of the Hail Mary during everyday family rituals, such as nursing or changing

a baby's diapers. Placing a baby in a crib or rocking an infant invites a parent to bless the child with a simple gesture, perhaps tracing the Sign of the Cross on the forehead in remembrance of Baptism. Such gestures are reminders of the parent's own pledge to grow in faith. A parent may simply whisper, "Keep us, O Lord, as the apple of your eye; shelter us in the shadow of your wings," as a child is prepared for sleep. Singing or humming a familiar hymn can also be relaxing and comforting for both parent and child.

HELP TOWARD FAMILY PRAYER

The presence of religious objects in the home helps families visually focus their prayer. "Parents should initiate their children at an early age into the mysteries of the faith of which they are the 'first heralds' for their children" (*Catechism*, 2225). The family Bible deserves a central place of reverence and should be easily accessible. Parents who develop the habit of reading and praying the Scriptures will grow in their knowledge and love of Jesus Christ and become stronger in their faith. In addition, a prayer corner in which an Advent wreath, Christmas crèche, the three Kings, a barren branch, a cross, a basket of colored eggs, a living plant, or a candle is placed at appropriate times will help mark the movement of the Church year. Perhaps a copy of the nuptial blessing can be displayed as a reminder of the prayerful beginning of the couple's married life. A yearly renewal of marriage vows in the children's presence can also call to mind the covenant of love that they share.

Belonging to a faith community helps form the family's prayer life. On visits to church, parents can make a point to take children to the Marian or Holy Family shrine. Such moments of quiet reflection in a peaceful and sacred place help parents acknowledge God's presence in the family.

Parents should initiate their children at an early age into the mysteries of the faith of which they are the "first heralds" for their children.

Catechism of the Catholic Church, 2225

CHURCH LIFE

A child's development in faith begins in the home. If values like justice, mercy, love, peace, and concern for the needs of others are going to be important in children's lives, they must see them routinely lived out by their parents.

THE FAMILY AND THE PARISH

It is important, however, that a parent seek the support of the parish community as the child grows in faith. Parents and children generally want to be warmly welcomed into the life of the parish, and the parish has an obligation to provide such a welcome. The presence and participation of young families in the life and worship of the faith community can be a sign of hope for all.

THE CHILD'S BAPTISM

Sometimes, preparation for the child's Baptism is a family's first formal contact with its parish. Uneasiness (perhaps because the family has not formally registered with the parish or from fear of being asked embarrassing questions) can mark this contact. Some parents are apprehensive because they have been away from the Church or because they are not sure what will be expected of them. Parents should not let such fears keep them and their child from entering or reentering the faith community. Simply contacting the parish for information about Baptism helps many parents experience a sense of welcome and belonging.

Most parishes offer helpful, realistic programs of baptismal preparation for parents. Specially trained couples help them prepare for their children's Baptism while sharing some practical ideas about nurturing the faith in young children.

Baptismal preparation programs can also help parents themselves grow in faith. Hearing from other parents and sharing their own concerns can strengthen their confidence in their ability to foster the religious development of their children.

The Baptism itself can be a prayerful and happy family celebration. The sanctity of the moment impresses itself on family members gathered to witness the baby's initiation into God's family. Underlying the importance of the community in the religious formation of children, three or four families usually present their infants for Baptism at the same time. Sometimes these Baptisms are celebrated at Mass with a larger congregation. "The whole ecclesial community bears some responsibility for the development and safeguarding of the grace given at Baptism" (*Catechism*, 1255).

The whole ecclesial community bears some responsibility for the development and safeguarding of the grace given at Baptism.
Catechism of the Catholic Church, 1255

At the Baptism, parents bestow the names they have chosen for their children and present them formally to be baptized. Parents mark them with the Sign of the Cross and seek their incorporation into the Body of the Church. They share the word of God with their children and renew the promises of their own Baptism. They accept the light of Christ into their homes and pledge that they will raise their children in the practice of the faith. Each of these actions signifies the presence of religious values in the family and sinks the roots of those values even deeper.

Godparents embody the responsibility shared by the entire Christian community to nurture the faith and to share in the religious development of children. In carefully choosing godparents who are good examples of Christian living, parents share the primary duty to nurture the child's faith.

FAMILY LIFE AND PARISH LIFE—A SACRED PARTNERSHIP

Sometimes parents become more involved in parish life as an immediate result of their child's Baptism. With the assistance of the pastor and the parish staff, they can be effective bridges to other parents in the years following their children's Baptism and before the children begin any formal instruction in religious values. This may, for example, take the form of preparing and sending out a brief prayer service for a home celebration on the first anniversary of Baptism. For the second anniversary, parents could send a brief article on sharing faith with two-year-olds to other parents of recently-baptized children.

Some parishes make even more frequent contact with new parents after Baptism.

Sometimes parents worry about taking infants or small children to church. They feel embarrassed when the baby cries or fidgets. Other members of the congregation should bear in mind how difficult it can be to calm a fussy child. Even if at first people seem upset by a baby's commotion, they are usually won over by a parent's smile that says, "He or she's only a baby." Perhaps, too, parents can suggest that the parish set aside a comfortable space where they can care for their children without disturbing the congregation, while still participating in Mass.

Besides joining in the celebration of the Sunday Eucharist, parents can develop other points of contact with the parish community. Parent groups on human sexuality or child development, parenting classes, and Christian Family Movement groups can be very practical and helpful. Some parents may also want to suggest to pastors and parish staff that they consider offering baby sitting co-ops and child care centers.

Some parents will want to become still more deeply involved in the parish community. Realizing that they teach values and transmit faith to their children by their example and their words, they may seek opportunities to learn more about their faith. Others may want to pray in small groups, in a parish RENEW program or a basic Christian community, or to join marriage support groups. Some welcome invitations to parish ministry as lectors, catechists, eucharistic ministers, cantors, ushers, ministers of care, parish council or education board members, etc.

Families usually need to feel that they belong to a community and to experience its hospitality before they are receptive to its efforts to provide support. Perhaps what families need most from their parishes are welcoming, prayerful, and beautiful experiences of the Sunday Eucharist, liturgies which readily lead parents and children to the Lord.

Reflection QUESTIONS

1. What special moments do I remember as I prepared for the birth of my child?

2. What do I think about when I am holding, feeding, or rocking my baby?

3. What experiences have I had with my baby that remind me of God's presence?

4. What moments in the life of my family lead me to praise and thank God?

5. What happy memories do I have of my child's Baptism?

Quotations
D O C U

You have asked to have your children baptized. In doing so you are accepting the responsibility of training them in the practice of the faith. It will be your duty to bring them up to keep God's commandments as Christ taught us, by loving God and our neighbor.

Rite of Baptism

For Christians a special gratitude is due to those from whom they have received the gift of faith, the grace of Baptism, and life in the Church. These may include parents, grandparents, other members of the family, pastors, catechists, and other teachers or friends.

Catechism of the Catholic Church, 2220

Inspired by the example and family prayer of their parents, children, and in fact everyone living under the family roof, will more easily set out upon the path of a truly human training, of salvation and of holiness.

Pastoral Constitution on the Church in the Modern World, 48

Fatherhood and motherhood are themselves a particular proof of love; they make it possible to discover love's extension and original depth. But this does not take place automatically. Rather, it is a task entrusted to both husband and wife. In the life of husband and wife together, fatherhood and motherhood represent such a sublime "novelty" and richness as can only be approached "on one's knees."

Pope John Paul II, Letter to Families, 7

from Church
M E N T S

Our Church must be an ally and advocate for parents as they struggle to meet their children's needs at home and in an often hostile world where powerful economic and social forces can overwhelm the love and care of a family.

Putting Children and Families First

The Christian communities to which the individual families belong or in which the children live also have a responsibility toward children baptized in the Church. By giving witness to the Gospel, living communal charity, and actively celebrating the mysteries of Christ, the Christian community is an excellent school of Christian and liturgical formation for the children who live in it.

Directory for Masses with Children, 11

The Rite of Baptism allows the Church to make the connection between the nuclear family and a larger family of believers responsible for the faith formation of an infant.

Putting Children and Families First

Infants who as yet are unable or unwilling to take part in the Mass may be brought in at the end of Mass to be blessed together with the rest of the community. This may be done, for example, if parish helpers have been taking care of them in a separate area.

Directory for Masses with Children, 16

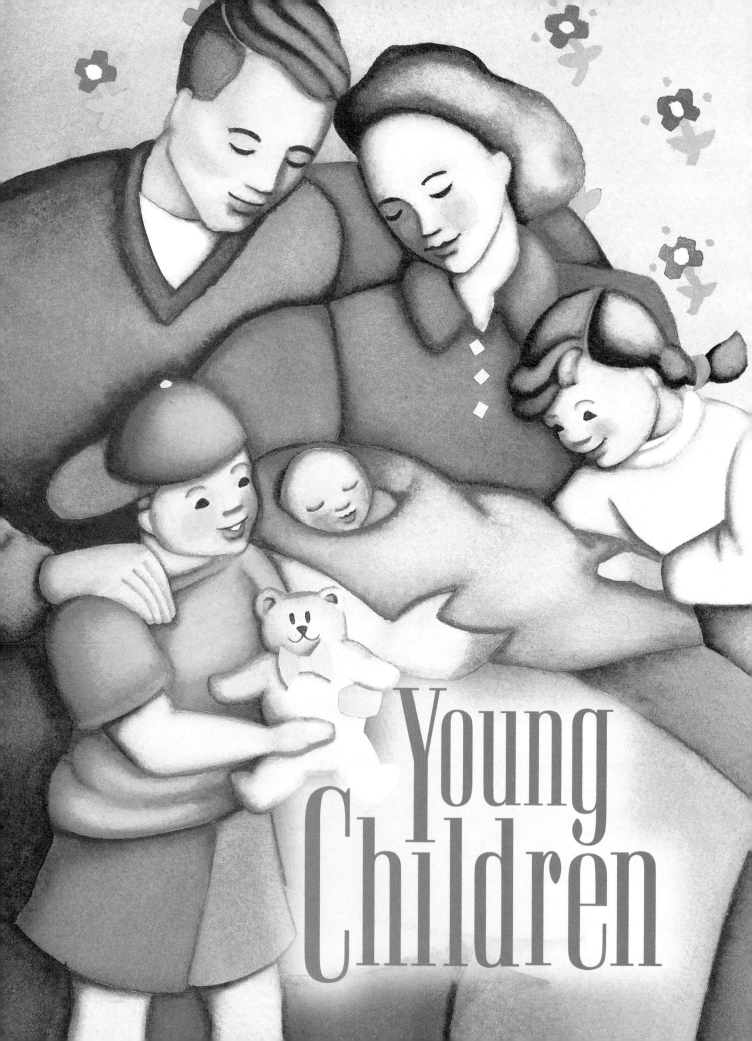

Young
Children

FAMILY LIFE

Young children between the ages of one and five are full of life and into everything. They are natural explorers who learn mainly through experience, not explanation. Their innate curiosity makes them eager to learn. Walking in the sunshine, hearing the crunch of fallen leaves underfoot, examining a snowflake, and feeling the splash of warm, spring rain on their faces—this is how children learn about the seasons.

Young children enjoy hands-on experiences, time to ask questions and tell stories, space for fantasy, opportunities to make mistakes, and chances to change. Their active imaginations involve them in a world of wonder and enchantment and prepare them to experience the mysterious presence of God in all of life.

THE POWER OF PARENTS

Human experiences can lay the foundations for a lifetime of religious growth and understanding. Every parental embrace builds a child's self-esteem. A parent folding an ill-tempered child into gentle arms teaches the child the meaning of forgiveness. Being loved enables the child to love. Reinforcing the experience of security within the family prepares children to trust in the abiding love of God.

In the everyday life of a family, parents exert a great influence over their children. "A wholesome family life can foster interior dispositions that are a genuine preparation for a living faith and remain a support for it throughout one's life" (*Catechism*, 2225). A parent's natural, unstudied love and concern provide a child with models of those values. A parent who celebrates the Sunday Eucharist with a child or who makes time for regular prayer at home affirms religious values in a way that has more impact than any formal teaching or preaching. Children will walk the way parents walk, not the way they point.

> A wholesome family life can foster interior dispositions that are a genuine preparation for a living faith and remain a support for it throughout one's life.
> *Catechism of the Catholic Church*, 2225

Language holds a particular fascination for young children. A parent's language profoundly affects them. A young child often imitates the tone, volume, and even vocabulary of a parent. Harsh words and raised voices can startle and confuse young children, while thoughtful words spoken with respect can strengthen their sense of security. If parents quarrel in front of their children, it is important that they also ask forgiveness and give signs of mutual acceptance in front of the children. In general, parents of young children can speak naturally and simply about God and their faith, as they do about other matters that they want their children to understand and appreciate.

which each member would have a chance to participate in decisions affecting all. When a parent involves a child in decision making (without, of course, abdicating parental responsibility) and suggests ways in which the child can contribute to family discussions, that child usually feels more valued and trusted.

GOD'S GIFT OF SEXUALITY

Sexual identity is an important part of a child's emerging sense of self. Sexuality, a gift from God, is naturally good; its development is a lifelong process that begins at birth. "Parents have the first responsibility for the education of their children" (*Catechism*, 2223). The encouragement of healthy self-concepts includes education in sexuality. Here, too, a parent's example teaches most effectively.

While children also receive information about sexuality from the media and from their contact with others, parents provide much of their child's early education in sexuality whether this is intended or not. A child notices, for example, when a parent treats other family members with respect, relates to them lovingly, and communicates with them affectionately.

Parents have the first responsibility for the education of their children.
Catechism of the Catholic Church, 2223

Parents encourage their children's trust, affirm their attempts to understand the world, and acknowledge their individual level of development when they show respect for their children's ideas and feelings. Young children sometimes take trivial matters very seriously or are deeply affected by what an adult might take for granted. More than anything else perhaps, children need parents who listen attentively to them.

In order to provide a real opportunity for family members to speak and listen to one another, a parent might suggest a weekly family meeting at

Children look to parents first for honest answers to their questions about their own bodies, the differences between the sexes, human reproduction in general, and the practical meanings of life-as-a-man and life-as-a-woman. If a parent views human sexuality as a gracious gift from God, the child will likely adopt the same view.

Parents can find help for education in sexuality from suitable reading and audiovisual materials or family life programs. The pastor, the parish director of religious education, the school principal, and the diocesan education and family life offices can provide specific suggestions and assistance for parents with young children. In light of their own experience, parents can make significant contributions to planning, presenting, and evaluating school and parish programs of education in sexuality and sexually-transmitted diseases. Once again, the diocesan education and family life offices can provide direction, assistance, and practical models for parental involvement in such programs.

THE YOUNG CHILD'S INTRODUCTION TO MORAL LIVING

Although young children are naturally self-centered, they can be encouraged to perform acts of kind ness and service. Even as the awareness of the rights and needs of others begins to develop, though, the child's natural attitude is: "What I want, I should have." Children are apt to be possessive and may try to get what they want with temper tantrums. At such times it is important for a parent to be firm and loving. To young children, "right" is what makes them happy or pleases the parent, and "wrong" is what makes them unhappy or displeases the parent.

Young children are capable of creativity and respond intuitively to signs and symbols. They have vivid imaginations, but abstract concepts like sin and justice are difficult for them to understand. When they take something that is not theirs or make up something that is not true, they usually do not relate their actions to external laws or even to objective definitions of "stealing" or "lying." They generally act to acquire what they want or protect themselves in a way that makes perfect sense to them. Nevertheless, parents need not only to discourage children from lying, stealing, and other unacceptable behaviors, but also to point out that some actions are morally good and others are not.

UNIQUENESS OF EACH CHILD

If there are older children in the family of the pre-schooler, they can become advisors and protectors as well as unique models of relationships that are sharing, forgiving, caring, and loving. As children interact, however, they may express jealousy and frustration as well. Young children find it hard to share a parent with brothers and sisters, even though the young ones ordinarily receive most of the parent's attention. Older children also need to be reassured that they have not been replaced in the parent's affection and are not less important now that they are not "cute" babies any more. Each child is a manifestation of God's love, and each needs the physical and emotional space that acknowledges his or her individuality and special relationship with a parent. Each child is a mystery, of whose individual gifts a parent needs to be aware.

THE POWER OF TELEVISION

Television and other media influence children's development. Even two-year-old children watch an average of 30 hours of television a week. TV has become the single most formative influence outside the family in shaping children's attitudes and values. Commercial television and advertising often emphasize the acquisition of possessions and brand-name clothing and communicate the message that what you have and wear is more important than who you are.

Parents need to decide very early how much they want television to affect their children and how much teaching they will permit TV to do. Violence on television, for example, shocks, confuses, frightens, and fascinates young children. Its impact on them should be minimized or controlled. Certain toys advertised on TV promote violence as an acceptable way of life. Sexually-explicit TV and movies convey a casual use of sex, debasing the sacred nature of an authentic loving relationship. A parent can watch television with a child and point out acceptable or unacceptable behavior presented on the screen.

A parent doesn't have to interrupt the program for a long lecture, but rather to say simply, "That's good," or "That's not so good," in response to different situations. Sometimes, of course, the parent best communicates sound values by changing the channel or turning off the set. However, the best way a parent can communicate appropriate values is by spending time with the child in some non-TV activity.

CELEBRATING FAMILY LIFE

Ordinary occasions at home provide opportunities to celebrate family life and God's presence at the heart of the family. Young children love hearing stories about their birth, seeing pictures of themselves at their Baptism, or hearing their recorded voice from some earlier occasion. "The home is well suited for *education in the virtues*" (*Catechism*, 2223). Family time around the supper table or a few moments alone with a parent before bed can become fond memories for children as they grow older. Such family experiences not only celebrate the love the family shares together, but also God's love for the family.

Experiences of joy, pain, hope, struggle, fulfillment, and disappointment can draw family members together in truly sacred moments. While at times it is difficult to see such routine experiences as holy, a moment's reflection makes it clear that the sacredness of all of life is present even in difficult experiences.

Special celebrations can become cherished family memories. Even if children cannot fully understand the religious significance of a particular occasion, such as Christmas, they enjoy hearing the stories and songs and are able to participate in the joy and love of the celebration and to sense that this time is special for the family. After a while, they might begin to ask, "Why don't we do this again?" or say, "We didn't do it that way last time." Special foods, times, places, and people convey a great deal of meaning for children. Such traditions help them learn that "our family is unique, and it is wonderful." Seasonal celebrations are good opportunities for families with specific ethnic traditions to tell their children of the importance of those traditions.

PRAYER LIFE

A young child's relationship with God grows along with the child's other relationships. Trust in a parent's loving presence and care gradually inclines the child to trust God. As children grow older, their image of God begins to become distinct from their image of a parent. Their innate sense of wonder and awe, along with the encouragement of a parent, prepares them for prayer.

LEARNING TO PRAY

All of us learn to pray by praying. Children learn to pray from a parent or from the other adults who care for them. If prayer is a routine experience in the home, the child can easily be included and given special parts as he or she becomes ready. A young child, for example, can take a turn at a simple task, such as leading a "Hosanna" or holding the Bible. While the presence of a child, like the presence of any other particular individual, will change the style of prayer in a family, the prayer remains the family's prayer, not a child's prayer in which others participate.

As children hear and see others around them pray, they want to pray as well. Learning to pray is an important part of religious formation, and a parent can encourage a child slowly according to his or her age and understanding. Children will sometimes want to speak or to listen to God in the company of the family and at other times alone.

The home is well suited for *education in the virtues.*
Catechism of the Catholic Church, 2223

Young children can learn to call upon the Father, Jesus, and the Holy Spirit. Starting out by providing a place of reverence for the family Bible, with a few moments of silence before a meal or sharing a few verses from a psalm at the beginning of the day, shows children that their parents value prayer and include prayer in the routine of the day.

MAKING TIME FOR PRAYER

Prayer, then, needs to be thought of as a companion to everyday life. Prayer at home should be as comfortable as a pair of old shoes, as familiar as the kitchen table. The home is the natural environment of prayer. Questions about the proper words, precise time, specific reason, or correct place for prayer are much less important than regarding prayer as an accepted and fundamental part of family life. Whatever forms and times for prayer seem naturally suited to a particular family's lifestyle are "right" for that family.

Most families have to struggle with busy schedules, constant demands, and the hectic pace of life in order to make time for regular prayer. Each family member will probably have to sacrifice an involvement or an activity so that the family can gather for prayer even once a day. If it is really important, though, the time will be found to slow down for prayer.

NATURAL TIMES FOR PRAYER

Because the family gathers naturally around the table for food, the table also becomes a place to see one another, to speak and listen to one another, and to share concerns. The moments before food is shared among family members can be opportunities to express dependence on those who prepared the food and upon God, who is the source of all nourishment. Even if all cannot be present, those who are present can still take their meal together. In this sense, family mealtime is sacred time.

Table prayer can take a variety of forms. The traditional Grace Before Meals, a few moments of silence, a special prayer written for a special occasion such as the day a child learns to ride a bike, a few words of praise and gratitude from each family member, or a gesture such as lighting a candle or joining hands are all forms of table prayer.

Bedtime prayer is an opportunity for a parent to help a child give thanks and praise to God for the gift of another day. For example, a parent might say, "Into your hands, O Lord, I commend my spirit," while tucking in the child. Some parents like to listen to their children saying the Lord's Prayer or simply to sit quietly together in God's presence before sleep. If parents value prayer, so will their children.

Pre-school children often use very concrete and sometimes humorous images in prayer. Their natural ease is often demonstrated by the abruptness with which they begin and end prayer, as well as their inclusion of a dog, or a doll, or an imaginary friend.

FORMAL AND INFORMAL PRAYER

Children need both formal and spontaneous prayer. Because they have frequent opportunities to repeat them with their children, parents are the best teachers of formal prayers like the Hail Mary and the Lord's Prayer. While very young children can learn the Sign of the Cross by heart, they should not be required to memorize longer prayers. Children usually enjoy reciting prayers with a parent.

Parents who share prayer in their own words make it clear that adults, as well as children, pray this way. For example, a parent may ask God's blessing for a particular person and invite the child to do the same for someone else.

A young child's prayer life can also be formed by listening to a parent share favorite stories. Fairy tales and other forms of children's literature may foster the religious value of hope. Parents can also tell the stories from the gospels in their own words and then ask the children to retell them in their own words. While children should not be expected to understand the religious meaning of the stories, they will learn in their way that the stories themselves are important to their parents. As they ask for repeated tellings, the meaning and details will come increasingly into focus for them.

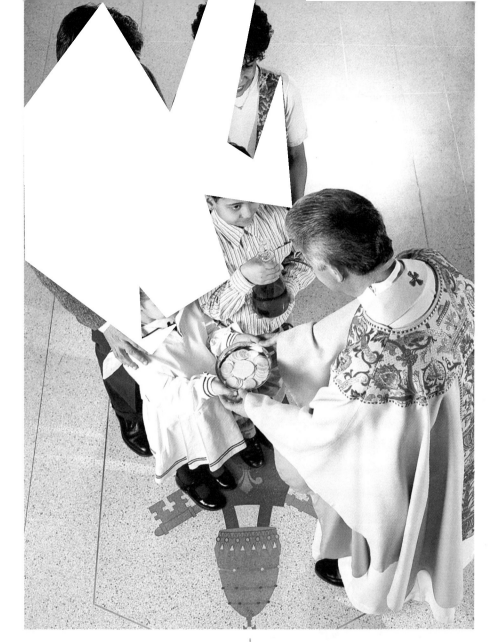

CHURCH LIFE

Faith, God's gift to each child, is shared initially, profoundly, and often unconsciously within the family. Although this sharing can seem awkward at first if one is not accustomed to it, parents can gradually come to feel at ease by telling their young children how they experience the Lord in people and in events. Even though formal activities and experiences outside the home are important in helping children grow in faith, the home remains the primary environment for learning religious values.

CHILDREN ARE PART OF THE CHURCH NOW

Young children learn such values by seeing them lived out. This is how they become aware that the Church is their community of faith, where people come together to worship God and serve others.

Children are not only the future of the Church; they are part of the Church now. If possible, they should know the pastor and the other parish ministers by name. Moreover, young children should be familiar with the church building before parents bring them to the Eucharist. At some quiet

time, when others will not be disturbed, parents should let them touch the altar, wander in the aisles, feel the holy water, smell the candles, examine the pictures or stained glass windows and the statues, and in general become comfortable in church.

Some parents are unsure when to take young children to Mass. Here are a few guidelines.

Even young children can understand the meaning of the Eucharist at their own level and the novelty of going to Mass also awakens the interest of some. But for others the experience is frightening or boring, especially if going to Mass is associated with frequent reminders to keep quiet or be still, along with threats, slaps, pokes, glares, or scowls. Since delight is so natural in young children, the gestures, drama, colors, sounds, sights, and movements of the liturgy have special significance for them. To encourage their sense of delight, it is helpful for the family to sit at the front of the congregation, close to what is taking place.

Children can learn simple responses and chants like "Amen" and "Alleluia." During reflective or listening periods, parents will need to hold them or distract them with a stuffed animal or book. But parents should direct children's attention to parts of the Mass that are capable of engaging their attention—various sounds, the offertory procession, the sign of peace. Family life is quietly yet beautifully manifested in the worshiping community when a parent carries or leads a child by the hand while receiving Holy Communion. If the priest or eucharistic minister blesses the child, the whole family's sense of belonging is reinforced.

When children do become distractions to other worshipers, it is best to take them out of church—preferably, if such is available, to a designated, supervised playroom or play area. When this happens, children should not be told they are being punished for bad behavior, while their good behavior in church is best encouraged by praise.

Thus a parent can help a child value going to Mass with the rest of the family and feel comfortable with the wider parish community. Occasional family and children's Masses are helpful: for example, a special family liturgy on Christmas Eve.

PRE-SCHOOL RELIGIOUS EXPERIENCE PROGRAMS

Some parishes or clusters of parishes provide religious experience programs especially for young children and their parents. Such programs usually seek to develop the religious awareness of young children and adults by calling their attention to the sacred as it is already present in their lives. Taking part in such a

program can prepare a child for participation in the larger parish community. In a supportive environment, parents and catechists can help young children explore, enjoy, and celebrate the wonders of God.

In some parishes, the early childhood program is offered at the same time as one of the Sunday Masses and its activities flow directly from the Sunday liturgy. Young children are brought into the church at the end of the Mass to be blessed along with the rest of the community. Parents are able to be more fully involved in the liturgy and have an opportunity for discussion with their children later.

The goal of such a program is to encourage the growth of the child's loving relationship with God and with the community of believers. This is done at a gentle pace, in ways suited to age, circumstances, and learning abilities. Young children are just beginning to expand their awareness of the larger world and to deepen their sense of wonder. A gradual development of religious understanding accompanies this human process.

The early childhood catechist can be a bridge linking parish and family. As a personal witness to Jesus, the catechist offers to assist both parent and child in their religious development. Catechists generally seek to build on parents' efforts by creating a loving and caring learning environment for both parents and children within the parish community. Early childhood programs of religious formation supplement the family and provide young children with additional influential models for developing attitudes, values, and behavior.

AT HOME IN CHURCH

Experienced parents can do a lot to see to it that their parishes make families with young children feel at home in the church and at the eucharistic celebration. They can suggest to the pastor and parish staff, for example, that the parish sponsor baptismal anniversary programs, baby-sitting co-ops, new parents' and single parents' support groups, child development groups, early childhood programs, and prayer groups for parents and young children. Sometimes, parent groups can sponsor celebrations for children and their families that appeal to the senses, involve the children, and are held at church, but are not part of Mass. Most important, parents can encourage the pastor and the other parish ministers to provide flexible programming that corresponds to the needs and realities of family life.

Reflection QUESTIONS

1. *On what occasions do I feel comfortable with my child in church?*

2. *How do I show respect for my child's feelings and ideas?*

3. *How do I help my child choose what to watch on television?*

4. *How do I make our home a comfortable setting for family prayer?*

5. *How does my child see me expressing my faith?*

Quotations

DOCU

Adequate pre-school, primary and secondary education is essential to full development of our children. Society at large is increasingly recognizing the effectiveness of Catholic schools in meeting the educational needs of children, including poor and minority children.
Putting Children and Families First

Sometimes, moreover, if the physical arrangements and the circumstances of the community permit, it will be appropriate to celebrate the liturgy of the word, including a homily, with the children in a separate, but not too distant, room. Then, before the eucharistic liturgy begins, the children are led to the place where the adults have meanwhile celebrated their own liturgy of the word.
Directory for Masses with Children, 17

Parents are the first and most important educators of their own children, and they also possess a fundamental competence in this area: They are educators because they are parents. They share their educational mission with other individuals or institutions such as the church and the state.
Pope John Paul II, *Letter to Families, 16*

The relationships within the family bring an affinity of feelings, affections and interests, arising above all from the members' respect for one another. The family is a *privileged community* called to achieve a "sharing of thought and common deliberation by the spouses as well as their eager cooperation as parents in the children's upbringing."
Catechism of the Catholic Church, 2206

from Church

MENTS

Parents must regard their children as *children of God* and respect them as *human persons*. Showing themselves obedient to the will of the Father in heaven, they educate their children to fulfill God's law.

Catechism of the Catholic Church, 2222

Families bring children to participate in the development of society. Parents help children grow in moral and spiritual maturity and also help to build a caring and just society.

Putting Children and Families First

The best catechesis in sexuality for children comes from the wholesome example of their parents and other adults.

National Catechetical Directory, 191

It is necessary to take great care that the children present do not feel neglected because of their inability to participate or to understand what happens and what is proclaimed in the celebration. Some account should be taken of their presence: for example, by speaking to them directly in the introductory comments and at some point in the homily.

Directory for Masses with Children, 17

Parents and others in intimate contact with infants and small children should speak naturally and simply about God and their faith, as they do about other matters they want their children to understand and appreciate.

National Catechetical Directory, 177

Primary Grade Children

FAMILY LIFE
THE CHILD AT A GLANCE

Six, seven, and eight year-old children often surprise their parents and teachers with how much they absorb and take to heart. Questions like, "Where do babies come from?," "Why did grandpa have to die?," "What do you eat and where do you sleep in heaven?," "Why do I have to be good?," "Is there really a God?," or "Why doesn't daddy live with us anymore?" come as easily as "Where did Santa buy his reindeer?" or "Where does the Easter bunny live?"

Children's natural sense of discovery, love of mystery, delight in ritual, and reverence for all living things are seeds from which religious values spring. Because they think in such concrete images, they express themselves in vivid language and colorful figures. In the primary grades they begin to form attitudes based largely on the attitudes they perceive in their parents and teachers. They also begin to notice differences between their family and other families.

Gradually they become more comfortable with the give and take of group activity and need less and less to be the center of everything. This growing sense of belonging to a community helps them practice sharing, forgiving, and kindness. With guidance, they later identify these values as Christian and learn to think critically, to make choices, and to discern right from wrong.

PARENTAL INVOLVEMENT IN FORMAL RELIGIOUS EDUCATION

Parents have a right and a duty to select the most suitable method of formal religious instruction for their children. In general, parents should give serious thought to a Catholic school if one is available, though in particular circumstances, they may choose a program of Catholic education outside a Catholic school. In either case, parents are not surrendering their children's religious formation to outsiders but are inviting teachers and catechists to become their partners. Regular communication and mutual support among parents, other significant family members, teachers, and catechists help to form a visible adult community of faith in which the children can grow.

Working parents, those who do not understand or have difficulty with English, or those who simply are shy may, however, have difficulty attending meetings and similar events. Participation might even be uncomfortable or embarrassing for them. Perhaps, then, those who attend such meetings could telephone those unable to attend and tell them what happened.

Sometimes parent and child both feel anxious when the child starts school. Parents should encourage children to see school as an extension of home.

In many ways, children represent the hopes and aspirations of their parents. Parents commonly want their children to be happier and more successful than they are themselves. Sometimes they even look to their children to accomplish what they could not—for example, success at sports, studies, or social life. Especially in these early years of schooling, however, children need to develop their own gifts at their own pace. Parents should refrain from comparing one child with another, pushing children into activities that do not appeal to them, and entertaining expectations that exceed a child's abilities.

Parents teach their young children respect for themselves and others by de-emphasizing competition. While competing with others helps children realize some of their potential, too much pressure to win teaches them that they are failures if they lose.

MAKING MORAL CHOICES

"Parents have a grave responsibility to give good example to their children" (*Catechism*, 2223). The behavior of children in the primary grades begins to mirror, in a specifically moral way, the behavior of parents and other significant adults. Children are quick to sense that a parent or another adult feels strongly about such things as lying or damaging another's property, even when they cannot understand the moral reasoning behind the judgments. They are more sensitive to the consequences of an act than they are to the morality of the act itself. For example, children know that taking something that does not belong to them must be wrong because they are usually punished if they are caught, but they are not sure why it is wrong to steal. It does not follow, however, that parents should not insist on morally good behavior until their children can supply the reasons for behaving in such a way. Parents must be especially careful to avoid teaching children that "it's only wrong if you're caught."

On the contrary, Christian parents need to share the traditional Christian values with their children by speaking about them clearly and frequently as well as by incorporating them into the actions of their own everyday lives. The Christian beliefs and practices, which parents hold faithfully and which the Church has traditionally taught, provide the framework in which children begin to make choices that are consistent with Christian values.

Children need practice in choosing among alternatives they face and giving reasons for their choices, for this is how they learn to think critically and make correct moral decisions. Parents should set up and consistently apply a flexible system for rewarding the acceptable and correcting the unacceptable. The key is consistency within loving and affirming family relationships.

Parents have a grave responsibility to give good example to their children.
Catechism of the Catholic Church, 2223

Each and everyone should be generous and tireless in forgiving one another for offenses, quarrels, injustices and neglect.

Catechism of the Catholic Church, 2227

FORGIVING AND SHARING IN THE FAMILY

Seeing other family members routinely seeking and offering forgiveness teaches young children to forgive and to accept God's loving forgiveness of them. "Each and everyone should be generous and tireless in forgiving one another for offenses, quarrels, injustices and neglect" (*Catechism*, 2227). Family life offers many opportunities for a parent to show forgiveness in ways a child can easily understand—a warm hug or honest words like, "You're forgiven," "I still love you," "Everything's okay," and "I'm not angry anymore." A parent's verbal and nonverbal expressions of genuine sorrow help teach a child how to apologize. The words "I'm sorry" are powerfully healing ones to speak and to hear.

Although members of a busy family can have trouble finding time for regular family meals, it is worth the effort. Families share much more than food at meals. The identity of the family itself is nurtured around the table. Children learn there to value the gathering of God's family around the table of the Eucharist. Distractions—television, telephone calls, visiting playmates—should be kept to a minimum at mealtime.

PRAYER LIFE
SPECIAL TIMES FOR ORDINARY PRAYER

While children begin their formal schooling at this age, ordinarily the home remains the most important setting for their experiences of prayer. As the day begins, the parent can encourage the child to offer a prayer of praise: for example, "Blessed are you, Lord, God of all creation," or "Jesus, my brother, you are the Light of the World."

In the evening, family members may signal their unity by holding hands while reciting the Lord's Prayer or one of the psalms, perhaps with a lighted candle to add a degree of solemnity. At bedtime the parent may wish simply to sit on the child's bedside, give a hug and say, "Peace be with you."

PERSONAL PRAYER

Children of this age are quite capable of learning to talk to God in their own words and to listen for God's message to them. They are easily encouraged to include their own thoughts and feelings in group prayer. They pray for pets and toys as readily as for parents and friends. Parents and teachers can help a great deal by reminding them of the beauty and wonder of God's creation, and by helping them to give thanks for the gift of life or a beautiful day and to petition for peace in their homes as natural responses to their life experiences.

SHARED PRAYER

At this age, too, children can be involved in the Church's liturgical prayer in a variety of ways with the pastor's approval. Simple celebrations that recall their own Baptism, uncomplicated group penance services, and participation at Mass provide opportunities for them to come to know Jesus present among them. Their sense of participation is enhanced by incorporating their own artwork, drama, or pageantry in prayerful celebrations.

Brief readings from children's translations of the Bible and stories drawn from the life of Jesus help children become familiar with the word of God at an early age. Selected stories from the Bible teach children the history of God's loving deeds and the faithful lives of God's chosen people. It is important for parents and teachers to adapt scriptural stories and readings from the psalms to seasonal celebrations such as Advent, Christmas, Lent, Easter, and Pentecost.

As a child becomes more curious about the Mass, a parent can answer questions, help the child follow the ritual movement of the priest or deacon, and teach the common responses made in the eucharistic liturgy. But the parent can also take the initiative in explaining the meaning of the various readings, prayers, and gestures. Repeating spoken responses, sung acclamations, and appropriate gestures during the Mass helps children feel at home in the worshiping community.

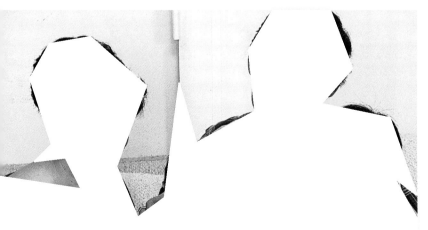

A parent can point out to a child that many human values are affirmed as the community celebrates the Eucharist. The natural desires to come together in a group, to be part of a group, to be welcomed and to welcome others, and to listen to others and be listened to by others are present in the worshiping community.

Seeking forgiveness, sharing greetings of peace, seeking nourishment, and expressing praise and thanks to God are profound human needs that find expression in the celebration of the Eucharist as well.

In faith, these human values reveal the profound religious meaning that lies beneath them. God is the source of forgiveness and peace. God's word and sacrament are nourishment for eternal life. God's love is the model for human love. Union with God is the goal of the worshiping community.

Primary grade children can learn how to pray together in community, whether it be the family, a class, or a parish group. First learned at home and at an earlier age, important prayers are reinforced in religion classes. While children should not be pressured to repeat formulas that they do not understand, memorizing traditional prayers is an important step on the way to integration into the formal prayer life of the community. This memorization should be adapted to the children's level and ability and introduced in a gradual and flexible manner. The best way for children to learn formal prayers is for parents to explain them and join the children frequently in praying them.

MANY KINDS OF PRAYER

Parents and teachers do well to see to it that singing, gestures, or a physical activity, such as a procession, accompany a prayer. Then children will more easily recall not only a prayer's words but its meaning and emotional tone. Besides the Sign of the Cross, the Our Father, the Hail Mary, the Glory to the Father and the Act of Contrition, children are able to learn simple acclamations, such as "Alleluia," and brief passages from Scripture, such as "The Lord is my shepherd. I shall not want."

The parish is the Eucharistic community and the heart of the liturgical life of Christian families; it is a privileged place for the catechesis of children and parents.

Catechism of the Catholic Church, 2226

There are several other forms of prayer that young children can appreciate and incorporate into their lives with help from parents and teachers. Reflective or centering silence, for example, is a form of prayer. Listening in silence to the inner presence of God helps children come to know that God's love dwells within and is sometimes communicated without words.

Music adds to the beauty of prayer and is often itself a form of prayer. Parents and teachers should expose children to the traditional forms of the Church's music and to sacred songs of their cultural tradition as well as contemporary musical forms specifically composed for them. Children's choirs and instrumental ensembles make it possible for them to lead and serve the worshiping community in the beautiful ministry of music.

Gestures that accompany sung or spoken prayer and taking part in simple dramatic presentations can also provide prayerful experiences for children. Religious art, stained glass windows, statues, and designs of the children's own making can enhance their prayer as well.

CHURCH LIFE
SACRED TIME AND SPACE

Because children develop an appreciation of the community beyond the family at this age, they need to experience the local parish community as a place of welcome and a sign of God's presence. "The parish is the Eucharistic community and the heart of the liturgical life of Christian families; it is a privileged place for the catechesis of children and parents" (*Catechism*, 2226). The sense of reverence for sacred time and space learned at home helps them feel at ease in the environment for prayer outside their homes.

Children enjoy becoming involved in choosing themes, readings, songs, symbols, and gestures for prayer services and liturgies. They are ordinarily delighted when invited to participate in dialogue homilies and usually share their feelings openly. When a eucharistic liturgy is celebrated, children can help prepare the altar with a cloth, flowers, banners, candles, and books. They can bring examples of their schoolwork or artwork forward during the offertory procession. Since they enjoy being involved and being of service, they could be encouraged to hold the cruets and carry a small processional cross and candles.

LEARNING OBJECTIVES FOR PRIMARY GRADE CHILDREN

Formal religion classes for primary grade children present Jesus as redeemer, brother, and friend. Through Jesus we are brought to the Father, the loving creator of everything, and to the Holy Spirit, the bond of love between Jesus and the Father, who gives life to the world today. In their first years of schooling, children also learn that the Church is the family of God and a

sign of Jesus' presence in the world. They learn that Mary, the mother of Jesus, is also their mother. By the example of her life, Mary's love for God nurtures their early growth in faith. In addition, the sacraments are presented to young children as signs of God's welcoming, nourishing, and forgiving love.

THE SACRAMENT OF RECONCILIATION

The experience of forgiveness and love in their own families prepares children to learn about the sacrament of Reconciliation. Formal instruction concerning the sacrament ordinarily begins in the first grade and continues throughout a child's school years.

Since parents have the right and the responsibility to direct the religious formation of their children, the pastor and parish staff should see that preparation for first reception of the sacrament of Reconciliation should involve them in meaningful ways. Parish programs should respect the readiness, age, ability, and circumstances of the children, as well as the intentions of the parents.

An important part of young children's preparation for the sacrament of Reconciliation is the opportunity to gather with classmates to plan simple services that celebrate God's willingness to forgive. They can meet and talk with the parish priest and, with the help of their parents, choose a confessor. The children also like to explore the reconciliation rooms in the church so that any unfamiliarity might be removed.

The Church's pastoral practice calls for the celebration of the sacrament of Reconciliation prior to the celebration of first Eucharist. Parish programs should clearly explain to parents that the Church's discipline in this regard grows out of its understanding of the sacrament as an experience of God's forgiving love. If, in an exceptional case, a child does not celebrate the sacrament of Reconciliation before first Holy Communion, he or she should not, on that account, be deprived of the Eucharist. In such an instance, the child should be encouraged to celebrate the sacrament of Reconciliation later and be given the opportunity to do so.

The goal of this preparation is to enable primary grade children to experience the sacrament of Reconciliation as an expression of God's personal love for them and for the whole community. Because conversion is a lifelong process that accompanies their growth in faith, children have a right to fuller instruction about the sacrament as they grow older.

In preparing primary grade children for the sacrament of Reconciliation, the concept of sin is presented to them in a way appropriate to their age level. Young children are not fully able to understand the impact of their actions. Their sense of responsibility is just beginning to develop. "Family catechesis precedes, accompanies, and enriches other forms of instruction in the faith" (*Catechism*, 2226). The things young children do might sometimes seem willful and deliberate, and their misdeeds are cause for concern. While children are capable of committing serious sin, they usually do not possess the level of moral judgment necessary to do so. Children should, however, be encouraged to express sorrow for their sins and to turn to God for forgiveness. Ongoing formation of

Family catechesis precedes, accompanies, and enriches other forms of instruction in the faith.
Catechism of the Catholic Church, 2226

conscience is a delicate matter for everyone, especially children. Sacred Scripture, the Church's tradition and teachings, and the light of the Holy Spirit assist each person to seek the truth, to seek what God wills.

Parents should be involved in determining a child's readiness to celebrate any sacrament. Usually parents do this in dialogue with the pastor or the member of the pastoral staff who is preparing the children. When children realize their need for forgiveness, understand that God's love and forgiveness are always available, realize their responsibility to do good and have an understanding of faith appropriate to their age, children are ready to celebrate the sacrament of Reconciliation.

If possible, the child's first experience of the sacrament of Reconciliation should occur within a carefully planned prayer service and there should be the option of speaking to the priest face to face or from behind a screen. Parish staff members are usually available to discuss these matters. Those involved in preparing children for this sacrament should ensure that its specific identity is kept distinct from the Eucharist by a clear separation in time and by unhurried planning.

THE EUCHARIST

According to their age and maturity, children should learn that the Eucharist is both a meal and a sacrifice. They can understand that Jesus invites them as his sisters and brothers to join him in the family meal which celebrates God's love for them and their love for God. They learn that the Eucharist is one of the sacraments of initiation. Even at this early age, they also can begin to appreciate that the Eucharist is a memorial and renewal of Jesus' sacrifice, the gift of himself on the cross. When the community gathers at Mass, it remembers and celebrates the saving death and resurrection of Jesus. Children quickly learn that Jesus offers himself to them as the Bread of Life in Holy Communion.

Reception of Holy Communion marks a turning point in a child's life. Besides signaling more active involvement in the community of believers, regular reception of Holy Communion fosters in the child a relationship with Jesus that is central to his or her religious development.

Children's first reception of the Eucharist joins them in table fellowship with the faith community. It ordinarily follows instructional preparation for both parents and children. A parent should try to be as involved as possible in any meetings, interviews, family activities, and parish celebrations that are offered. Children will want to tell their parents what they are learning about the Eucharist in school and will ask many questions as well. Preparing for First

Communion with children enables parents to deepen their understanding and appreciation of the Eucharist. Their involvement in preparation programs demonstrates not only that they love their children but also that they value the Eucharist and the growth of their own faith life.

When a parent in dialogue with the pastoral staff determines that the child can tell the difference between ordinary bread and the Eucharist, has a knowledge of faith appropriate to his or her age level, and expresses a desire to receive Jesus, the child is ready for the first reception of the Eucharist. Parish staff members, catechists, and teachers are generally available to discuss this readiness with parents and make suggestions.

Since First Communion, for most families, is such an important occasion, parents need to remain clearly focused on its spiritual significance rather than on secondary concerns like receiving gifts, buying clothes, or planning parties.

A parent's own attitude toward the Eucharist significantly influences the attitude of the child. Parents who celebrate the Eucharist each Sunday teach its value to their children more profoundly than any teacher or catechist ever could. The experience of assisting children in preparing for and celebrating First Communion can be an occasion for the renewal or awakening of a parent's faith as well.

Parents of unbaptized children also can feel reassured by the Church's caring and thoughtful approach to the child's initiation into the Church. Such initiation, which occurs within the supportive embrace of the parish community, leads to the celebration of the sacraments of Baptism, Confirmation, and Eucharist. During the children's preparation time (called the "catechumenate for children"), the seed of faith of the young child is nurtured and sustained. How wonderful it is for a parent to respond to the grace of the Holy Spirit and present a child for entrance into the faith community in this way. Indeed, a parent's faith may be strengthened and result in a heightened commitment (or re-commitment) to the Christian way of life.

Reflection
QUESTIONS

1. *How did I feel the day my child started school? How did my feelings change?*

2. *Why does my child still love me even though I make mistakes?*

3. *What does my child do or say that reminds me of myself at that age?*

4. *What activities and interests do I have to give up so that I can spend time with my family?*

5. *How is forgiveness shared in our family?*

6. *How do I help my child experience family meals as opportunities to share life and love?*

Quotations

DOCU

In order to overcome today's widespread individualistic mentality, what is required is a concrete commitment to solidarity and charity, beginning in the family with the mutual support of husband and wife and the care which the different generations give to one another. In this sense the family too can be called a community of work and solidarity.

Pope John Paul II, Encyclical on the 100th Anniversary of "Rerum Novarum," 49

In the family, ... special attention must be devoted to the children by developing a profound esteem for their personal dignity and great respect and generous concern for their rights.

Pope John Paul II, On the Family, 26

It is therefore urgent to promote not only family policies, but also those social policies which have the family as their principal object, policies which assist the family by providing adequate resources and efficient means of support, both for bringing up children and for looking after the elderly....

Pope John Paul II, Encyclical on the 100th Anniversary of "Rerum Novarum," 49

Parents as well as those who take their place are obliged and enjoy the right to educate their offspring; Catholic parents also have the duty and the right to select those means and institutions through which they can provide more suitably for the Catholic education of the children according to local circumstances.

The Code of Canon Law, Canon 793, 1

from Church
M E N T S

Parents' respect and affection are expressed by the care and attention they devote to bringing up their young children and *providing for their physical and spiritual needs*. As the children grow up, the same respect and devotion lead parents to educate them in the right use of their reason and freedom.

Catechism of the Catholic Church,
2228

It is necessary to take great care that the children do not feel neglected because of their inability to participate or to understand what happens and what is proclaimed in the celebration. Some account should be taken of their presence, for example, by speaking to them directly in the introductory comments and in part of the homily.

Directory for Masses with
Children, 17

The commandment of the Decalogue calls for a child to honor its father and mother. But...that same commandment enjoins upon parents a kind of corresponding or symmetrical duty. Parents are also called to honor their children, whether they are young or old. This attitude is needed throughout the process of their education, including the time of their schooling.

Pope John Paul II,
Letter to Families, 16

No institution is more deeply involved in serving the needs of children than our community of faith. We bring not only deep conviction, but also vast experience to the challenge of meeting the needs of children.

Putting Children and Families First

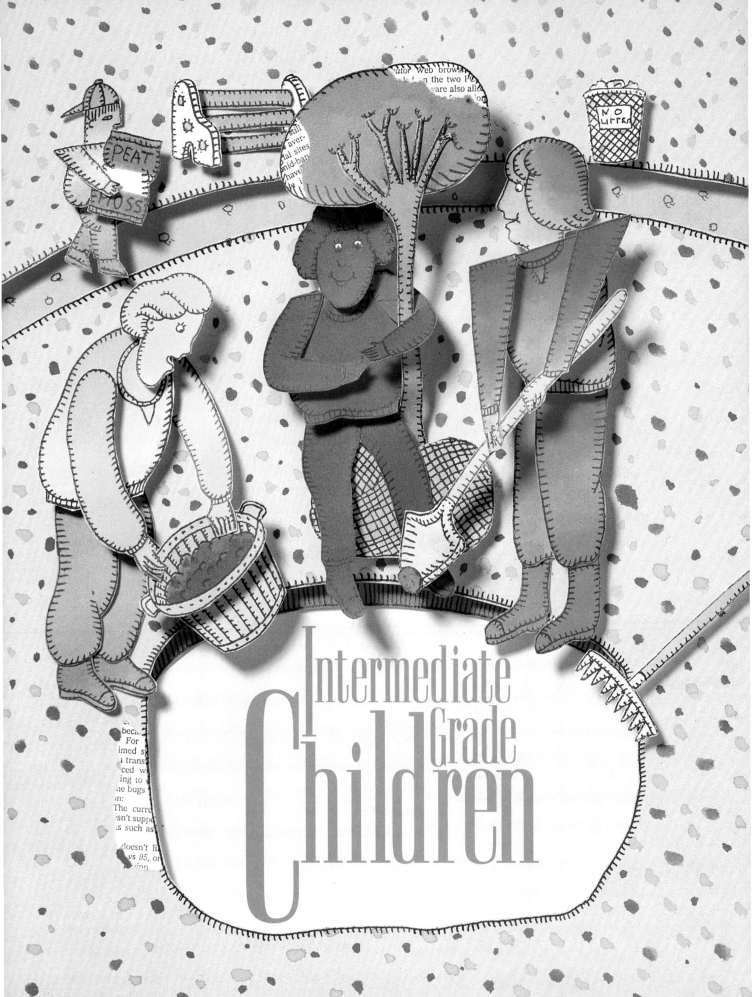

Intermediate Grade Children

FAMILY LIFE

Nine, ten and eleven year-old children like to show their parents how grown up they have become. "Jimmy" may suddenly prefer being called "Jim." Beth may want to walk somewhere with a group of friends rather than be driven. Intermediate grade children may start coin collections, originate secret clubs among their friends, or really throw themselves into a project at school. They will begin to question standard family routines and often ask "why"— why they have to make their beds before they go to school, why some children do not have enough food to eat, or why someone doesn't seem to like them.

> Children in turn contribute to the *growth in holiness* of their parents.
> *Catechism of the Catholic Church, 2227*

Questions are normal and healthy signs of a child's development. Children at this age are beginning to think abstractly. For instance, they begin to see that each family member's help and cooperation are needed to keep the house in order. They can relate people and events to one another. A sense of history gradually develops. They begin to appreciate what loyalty and honesty mean. They are capable of reflecting on their own actions and of realizing what effects their actions may have on others.

Children in the intermediate grades want very much to be included in family discussions. They are able to make genuine contributions. Family meetings provide the members with opportunities to share feelings, discuss difficult issues, plan vacations, or decide on major purchases. Families accustomed to such discussions usually can manage conflicts and defuse the build-up of anger and resentment among their members. Being listened to fosters a sense of self-worth and encourages responsibility in children. A parent's confidence helps the child feel a sense of belonging and importance within the family. At times, a child can give needed support to a parent, too. "Children in turn contribute to the *growth in holiness* of their parents" (*Catechism*, 2227).

DISCIPLINE

Children in the intermediate grades need boundaries. Discipline includes everything that a parent does to help a child learn to act properly. It involves the encouragement of acceptable behavior and the restriction of unacceptable behavior. Normally, the reasons for disciplinary measures should be explained to children. Explanations should be understandable and given in a manner that fosters self-esteem. The goal in disciplining children is to help them become self-disciplined. Consistent discipline lets children know that parents care about them and want to help them reach this goal. It also helps them learn that actions have consequences.

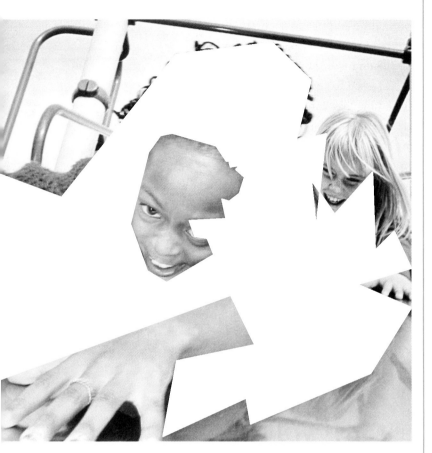

the explanations that children give for their behavior in order to avoid judging and acting unfairly. Admitting a mistake, when one is made, and asking forgiveness are healthy things to do.

GIVING CHILDREN WINGS
Intermediate grade children begin to test their competence and independence in a variety of ways—joining a team, going places with friends, having a "best" friend, and so on. They become more and more sensitive to the judgments and standards of peers and fear being "left out" by their friends. This can cause a parent some concern.

Without becoming overprotective, parents must be alert to people or experiences that can harm their children. Children sometimes test the ideas of peers against the ideas of a parent, even though they desire the parent's understanding and approval. This new influence of peers can confuse children.

SPEAKING OF SEX
During the latter part of children's intermediate years, their developing bodies heighten their awareness of sexuality. They are inquisitive about their own bodies, as well as those of others. In order to test reactions, they sometimes begin to do things to

Threats of punishment or reward that are not carried out confuse children and weaken parental authority. Children need to know what to expect when they conform to family expectations, alter those expectations just a little, or disregard them entirely.

Whatever positive and effective methods of discipline are chosen by families, children need to know that a parent can both forgive and forget. Children learn discipline best from parents who are self-disciplined. Since parents are human, however, they will sometimes overreact or misjudge. Although this is normal, still parents should pay attention to attract the attention of the opposite sex. Because of the explicit way in which sex is treated in movies, TV shows, music videos, and magazines, children have more knowledge of sexually-related things than they actually understand. At times they pretend to know everything about sexuality and sexually-related diseases, while knowing very little. Birth control and the use of condoms are examples of this. Children would like their parents to create a comfortable setting for them to learn more about human sexuality and to appreciate it as good and normal. For example, parents may teach children that the virtue of chastity requires abstinence from sexual expression outside of marriage. Parents need to teach their children that it is wrong to engage in sexual activity before the faithful bond of Christian marriage has been established. They need to know from an early age that chastity is a virtue to be practiced by all Christians, young and old, single or married. They need to know that human sexuality is a profound mystery and that there is no such thing as safe or casual sex.

Children want a parent to be open to talk about sexuality. Their feelings, questions, and doubts are very confusing to them. "Since boys and girls at puberty are particularly vulnerable to *emotional influences*, through dialogue and the way they live, parents have the duty to help their children resist negative outside influences that may lead them to have little regard for Christian formation in love and chastity. Especially in societies overwhelmed by consumer pressures,

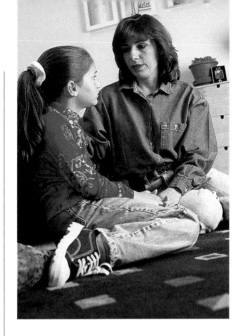

parents should sometimes watch out for their children's relations with young people of the opposite sex—without making it too obvious. Even if they are socially acceptable, some habits of speech and conduct are not morally correct and represent a way of trivializing sexuality, reducing it to a consumer object. Parents should therefore teach their children the value of Christian modesty, moderate dress, and, when it comes to trends, the necessary autonomy characteristic of a man or woman with a mature personality" (*The Truth and Meaning of Human Sexuality*, 97).

To foster healthy attitudes toward sexuality, a parent should turn for help to outside sources, such as parish meetings on human sexuality, approved parenting programs, and printed materials recommended by the parish or diocesan education office. Education in sexuality provides a good opportunity for parents, teachers, and other adults to teach children that sexuality is a gift from God to be cherished and nourished throughout life.

For the most part, intermediate grade children still look to their parents when they need advice. They will ask *why* things are right or wrong, not just *what* is right or wrong. Parents should encourage this. Children sometimes turn to older brothers or sisters, a cousin, a teacher, a coach, a neighbor, or perhaps a grandparent. While parents may feel offended, it is natural for children of this age to look for some other confidant. At the same time, communication between parents and children needs to remain open, honest, consistent, and trusting.

CONTROLLING THE TUBE

Television exerts a powerful influence on children. It has been held responsible for many of society's problems because of its presentation of violence, explicit sex, and questionable values. Although some sense a decline in the violence shown in public programming, research indicates that watching violent television programs can cause children to become too aggressive as well as to become less sensitive to real life tragedies. Sometimes they are confused by the unrealistic view of life TV offers. When television programs are chosen carefully,

however, they can be healthy influences on the development of children. Programs that appeal to all members of the family can inform children in delightful ways, while drawing the family together.

Advertising, too, often creates artificial expectations about life that children tend to take literally at this age. Parents should teach children to be skeptical of advertising and critical of the consumerism it promotes. For example, while watching a commercial with a child, a parent might simply remark that all persons have dignity and value because they are made in the image of God, not because of their possessions.

Although it takes considerable effort, parents can control the influence of television in children's lives. A parent's own viewing habits—what and how long—

disclose how he or she really feels about television. The parent needs to become familiar with the programs the child wants to watch. From time to time, the parent should watch with the child, talk about the issues that are presented, and answer questions that arise. A parent also needs to set limits on the time for TV watching and the programs to be watched. Naturally, a parent needs to do the same with other media—videos, CDs or tapes, computer games, radio, books, magazines, newspapers.

SHARING THOUGHTS AND FEELINGS ABOUT DEATH

Children are generally curious about death. By the time they reach the intermediate grades, they have probably suffered the loss of a grandparent, a neighbor, or at least a favorite pet. They know how to "play dead" in their games and will openly ask about death.

While adults often have difficulty discussing death, a parent's attitude influences a child more than words. Examples from nature—the changing seasons, dead leaves, even a dead goldfish—can deepen the child's understanding of the mystery of death. Parents must make thoughtful decisions about when to take children to wakes, funerals or memorial services, but children should definitely be part of their own families' experience of grieving at the deaths of loved ones.

While children's grief is different from the grief of adults, they should be given the opportunity to say good-bye to deceased relatives and friends. When a parent can express his or her own emotions about death appropriately, a child's tears and lonesome feelings about the loss of a loved one can surface freely and can be discussed more easily.

Remembering those who have died helps children realize that, even in death, they are still a part of life. Visits to the graves of deceased relatives and friends, keeping their pictures close at hand, and encouraging the children's questions about them provide good opportunities to deal with the mystery of death.

A parent's firm trust in the resurrection can teach a child that death is not an end, but a beginning. It is the link between life on earth and life in the fullness of Christ. The resurrection of Jesus is central to Christian faith and frees the Christian from excessive worry about death. The image of the cross can be presented as a powerful sign of hope to children because it represents Jesus' triumph over sin and death as well as his promise that we, too, will rise.

PRAYER LIFE

Family prayer for intermediate grade children should involve them in more responsible ways and continually invite them to reflect on their own importance in the family. For example, as part of the family's prayer in the evening, the child might read Mary's Song of Praise (Luke 1:46–55) or lead a familiar song.

SPECIAL TIMES FOR SPECIAL PRAYER

Gatherings for birthdays, anniversaries, graduations, engagements, marriages, deaths, and many other events provide special occasions for children to join and sometimes lead the family in prayer. Children are usually willing to share their personal prayers with others. They are pleased to join in the table prayers, adding their needs to family prayers of petition and mentioning their own thanks to God. They also still enjoy personal moments of prayer with a parent.

At this age, children can plan and lead simple prayer services for their families and classmates. All it takes is a chosen reading from Scripture, a brief period of quiet, praying a psalm or singing a simple song, an opportunity for some shared reflections on the reading, and perhaps saying together the Lord's Prayer.

SEASONS OF THE CHURCH YEAR

Such prayer services are especially appropriate for special family occasions as well as for marking the seasons of the Church year. For example, during Advent, when darkness comes early in the evening and Christians look for Jesus who dispels darkness, prayerful waiting is the dominant theme. Gathering for prayer each evening at the Advent wreath and lighting a new candle on each of the four Sundays of Advent help the family mark the Advent season. Then Christmas gives us the chance to delight in recalling God's promise to love us with an abiding love. Families gather to join hands and bless their Christmas tree or Nativity scene.

Sharing cultural traditions and family rituals and retelling familiar Christmas stories deepen family bonds in the context of a profound religious event. At the Epiphany, which concludes the Christmas season, some families form a procession, as did the Three Kings, and move through the house, blessing the rooms as they go.

During Lent we focus on the passion and death of Jesus, while looking forward to his resurrection. Traditional Lenten practices are fasting, prayer, and sharing. A family might try to live on a poverty budget one day each week and share with a food pantry the food that would ordinarily be eaten. A cross or barren branch might mark the place of family prayer, while the prayer itself empha-

sizes reflective silence. Sharing time with the sick, the elderly, the physically or intellectually challenged, shut-ins, or prisoners is also a way to give alms to the poor. "The duty of making oneself a neighbor to others and actively serving them becomes even more urgent when it involves the disadvantaged, in whatever area this may be." (*Catechism*, 1932).

Holy Thursday, Good Friday, and the Vigil of Easter are the most important days of the Christian year. They mark the Passover of Jesus—his passage from death to life, his passion, death, and resurrection. The richness of the liturgy's symbolism makes sharing the Body and Blood of Jesus on Holy Thursday, commemorating his passion and death on Good Friday, and keeping the night watch of the resurrection on the Easter Vigil powerful family experiences.

The Easter season celebrates Jesus' triumph over death with symbols of abundant life and beauty. Prayer often adopts the liturgical signs: baptismal water, Easter fire, and the Easter candle. Joyous singing of the "Alleluia" and renewal of baptismal promises can be incorporated into the family's prayer at home. Family gatherings for prayer may focus on the renewal of creation in the spring symbolized by colored eggs, sprouting bulbs, and the warm seasonal rain. Planting seeds, cultivating the soil, raking winter debris, or spring housecleaning can lead families to a deeper awareness of the renewal of Christian life that they celebrate in the resurrection of the Lord.

May traditionally is Mary's month. It is a good time for short family outings—pilgrimages, really—to nearby shrines of Our Lady, for setting up May altars in the home, and for praying the family Rosary.

At Pentecost we celebrate the presence of the Holy Spirit in our lives and in the Church. Wind and fire are two signs associated with God's Spirit from the earliest times. Standing in a breeze or watching a bonfire can lead children to reflect on the mysterious nature of these elemental symbols. Repeating the phrase "Come, Holy Spirit" can help focus the family's prayer at this time of year.

SILENT PRAYER

At this age children need time for peaceful pondering, and a period of reflective silence is an appropriate part of a prayer service or can be prayer itself. Children are capable of meditating on God's word or action in their lives, so it can be helpful to offer a thought from Scripture—for example, "I am the vine and you are the branches"—for their reflection.

The duty of making oneself a neighbor to others and actively serving them becomes even more urgent when it involves the disadvantaged, in whatever area this may be.

Catechism of the Catholic Church, 1932

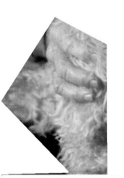

CHURCH LIFE

The personal witness of adults gathered as a worshiping community encourages children to grow in faith. Children sense that the sacraments bind the family of God more closely together. Regular worship in well-known surroundings with friendly people according to a familiar ritual helps children feel at home.

Children at this age enjoy taking more responsibility in planning their own liturgies, preparing the space for prayer, and performing some of the liturgical roles. Acting out Scripture stories, role playing the lives of the saints, and doing religion projects appeal to them because they enjoy working in small groups.

CHILDREN CAN GIVE TOO

Children often become enthusiastic about helping out, and service to others usually appeals to them. A parent can develop the concept of service by encouraging a child to perform acts of kindness within the family and in the neighborhood. For example, children can

- help collect food for the hungry
- assist younger children with school work
- visit elderly neighbors
- raise money for the missions
- make baptismal garments for infants of the parish
- accompany a eucharistic minister on a visit to a sick person
- send a card to a candidate for Confirmation
- participate in a car wash to raise funds for a special project.

TRADITIONAL PRAYER

Traditional prayers are best reviewed and refreshed through regular use within the family. Sometimes the family may wish to say the rosary together, while at other times individual family members may wish to pray it by themselves. At this age also children are able to learn the meaning of the words of both the Nicene Creed, normally used at Mass, and the Apostles' Creed, which can be used at Masses with children, while increasing their familiarity with the wonderful prayer book of the psalms. The psalms were composed for every kind of life situation. Those which express praise and thanksgiving are particularly appropriate for helping families express shared experiences.

Service activities make a deep impression on children of this age, especially when they have opportunity to reflect on their experiences and write and pray about them.

LEARNING OBJECTIVES FOR INTERMEDIATE GRADE CHILDREN

In formal catechetical programs, intermediate grade children deepen their understanding of the sacraments of initiation (Baptism, Confirmation, Holy Eucharist), healing (Reconciliation, Anointing of the Sick), and the sacraments in service of communion (Matrimony, Holy Orders). They learn that the Church is the Body of Christ of which they are important members. They become more familiar with the liturgical seasons.

Formal religious education in the intermediate grades focuses on a deeper understanding of the Trinity. The Father creates and orders all that exists; the Son is the Savior of all; and the Spirit sanctifies the world. Presented for the first time are the history and formation of God's word, the Bible, the development of the people of God, and the story of the covenant relationship by which God binds himself to his people in love.

Flowing from that covenant relationship is the Law, part of which is summarized in the Ten Commandments of the Old Testament and the Two Great Commandments of the New. The Ten Commandments express God's love by challenging us to use freedom responsibly. The Two Great Commandments focus the life of the Christian on love for God and love for others. Children learn that the way we live expresses our love for God, who shares life and love with us.

Jesus is presented as the model of Christian life, the heroic redeemer and reconciler who leads all people to God. Children learn that Jesus is at once fully God and fully human, and that he carried out his mission to bring God's love to us even though it meant his death. Through the Holy Spirit, they come to know Jesus as he is present in Scripture and tradition, in the Church and the sacraments, and in the other persons of faith.

CHRISTIAN MORALITY FOR INTERMEDIATE GRADE CHILDREN

Children of this age gradually become more sensitive to the consequences of their actions. For example, whereas before they may have refrained from stealing because they feared being caught, now their sense of fairness and their dislike of the atmosphere of suspicion, which stealing breeds, serve as deterrents.

A more formal introduction to Christian morality is needed now. Parents and teachers should present Christian moral principles as positive norms for living and should encourage children to observe, explore, interpret, choose, and make judgments in their light. They should help their children to form their consciences correctly, in keeping with the teaching of the Church. Parents

should challenge their children to give practical expression to the virtues of faith, hope, and love. Children readily understand that God has initiated a loving relationship with us and that we are God's loving people. This is also a time for developing a deepened sense of the beauty and importance of Reconciliation, as a sign of God's love and forgiveness which we share in the Church.

They also have no trouble grasping that fidelity, reverence, justice, peace, mercy, and compassion are among the established norms of Christian life, and that this life is not only modeled on Jesus' life but is a participation in it. So, for example, the Beatitudes can be explained as examples of positive gospel values. There should be consistent emphasis on the fact that Jesus' challenge to love is a call to generous service and concern for others.

At this time, too, children should be encouraged to respect the beliefs of other religious groups. They can learn to be tolerant of various faith traditions yet still be proud of their Catholic faith and identity.

They can learn to develop a positive attitude toward people who are sincere in their convictions and an appreciation of the elements of goodness and truth in their beliefs.

LEARNING BY WATCHING

Children learn morality from the behavior and attitudes of adults whom they love or upon whom they depend. Their ability to think critically, distinguish right from wrong, and choose what is right develops within the context of consistent, caring relationships with parents, teachers, and other adults.

At this age, when they are just beginning to make personal decisions based on reasoned judgments, children are still very likely to imitate those whom they respect. They find it confusing when, for example, knowing that stealing is wrong, they see mother or father bringing home office supplies that belong to the company and putting them to personal use. Nor are they any more comfortable with ambiguity. For them an action is either right or wrong. There is no "in-between."

Reflection QUESTIONS

1. *What do I usually say and do to affirm my child?*

2. *What qualities do my child's friends exhibit?*

3. *How do I use television to teach my child?*

4. *How do we celebrate the seasons of the Church year in our family?*

5. *How do I help my child choose from several alternatives?*

Quotations

This growing culture of violence reflected in some aspects of our public life and entertainment media must be confronted. But it is not just our policies and programming that must change, it is our hearts. We must condemn not only the killing but also the abuse in our homes, the anger in our hearts, and the glorification of violence in movies and music.
Confronting a Culture of Violence

Through families, children should come to identify with the most needy in the community, especially poor and suffering children, and should develop a life-long commitment to respond through service to the poor and disadvantaged and through action for justice and peace in their own communities and the world.
Putting Children and Families First

Our entertainment media too often exaggerate and even celebrate violence. Children see 8,000 murders and 100,000 other acts of violence on television before they leave elementary school.
Confronting a Culture of Violence

In our society, we need to resist the trends toward excessive individualism, materialism, and the quest for personal pleasure above all else. Real happiness and satisfaction come from who we are and how we care for one another rather than from what we have.
Putting Children and Families First

Families bring children to participate in the development of society. Parents help children grow in moral and spiritual maturity and also help to build a caring and just society
Putting Children and Families First

from Church

M E N T S

The parents' love is also the animating principle and therefore the norm inspiring and guiding all concrete educational activity, enriching it with the values of kindness, constancy, goodness, service, disinterestedness and self-sacrifice that are the most precious fruit of love.

Pope John Paul II, On the Family, 36

As many children as possible should have special parts in the celebration, for example: preparing the place and the altar, acting as cantor, singing in the choir, playing musical instruments, proclaiming the readings, responding during the homily, reciting the intentions of the general intercessions, bringing the gifts to the altar, and performing similar activities in accord with the usage of various communities.

Directory for Masses with Children, 22

Even in Masses with children, "silence should be observed at the proper time as part of the celebration" lest too great a role be given to external action. In their own way children are genuinely capable of reflection. They need, however, a kind of introduction so that they will learn how to reflect within themselves, meditate briefly, or praise God and pray to God in their hearts, for example after the homily or after communion.

Directory for Masses with Children, 37

The use of pictures prepared by the children themselves may be useful, for example, to illustrate a homily, to give a visual dimension to the intentions of the general intercessions or to inspire reflection.

Directory for Masses with Children, 36

Young
Adolescents

FAMILY LIFE

Suddenly (or so it seems to many parents) children turn twelve or thirteen and become young adolescents. They are beginning an exciting but not infrequently painful stage. Parental love and support are especially necessary to them in their self-discovery. Young adolescents are experiencing change in almost every aspect of their lives, but that change brings growth. Adolescence provides them with many happy experiences but also many that are intensely confusing.

Each young adolescent develops at his or her own pace; they vary widely in maturity and ability. Physical growth is rapid and bodily changes are quite dramatic. Emotions can range from spontaneous joy and playfulness to periods of self-doubt and discouragement. Awkwardness and self-consciousness are typical.

CHANGING BODIES, CHANGING HEARTS

It is normal for young adolescents to be quite sensitive and insecure, because the mystery of their emerging sexuality bewilders them. They are trying to incorporate their bodily changes and maturing emotions into their developing self-image. Social pressure sometimes adds to their confusion by prematurely hastening or intensifying relationships with members of the opposite sex. A parent faces the dual task of encouraging healthy boy/girl relationships and of saying no to what is inappropriate or wrong.

Parents should speak plainly and openly about the virtue of chastity to their adolescent children. "In answering *children's questions*, parents should offer well-reasoned arguments about the great value of chastity and show the intellectual and human weakness of theories that inspire permissive and hedonistic behaviour. They will answer clearly, without giving excessive importance to pathological sexual problems. Nor will they give the false impression that sex is something shameful or dirty, because it is a great gift of God who placed the ability to generate life in the human body, thereby sharing his creative power with us. Indeed, both in the Scriptures (cf. *Song of Songs* 1–8; *Hosea* 2; *Jeremiah* 3:1–3; *Ezekiel* 23, etc.) and in the Christian mystical tradition, conjugal love has always been considered a symbol and image of God's love for us" (*The Truth and Meaning of Human Sexuality*, 96). Especially in light of what they see and hear in the media, adolescents need to know that abstaining from sexual activity is a positive value in their lives. They need to know that the permanent and faithful relationship of Christian marriage is the proper context of sexual expression.

To help young adolescents become comfortable with their sexuality, parents generally have to be comfortable with their own. Young people need the good example and good advice of responsible adults who have achieved security and confidence about their own sexuality. They also need the correct information at the appropriate time about the human body, reproduction, and responsible use of the gift of sexuality. They need to discuss ways of expressing closeness and what it means to feel "special" about someone. Education in sexuality is learning for a lifetime.

When young adolescents question family rules and what they perceive as injustice, they need guidance from a parent, as well as time and space to reflect on their own thoughts and feelings. By and large, most young adolescents value and respect their parents and family, but it is not uncommon at this stage for defiance and disrespect to color their response to parental authority.

Young adolescents search for ways to belong to the group or to the family. They try to build solid friendships with peers. They can truly sympathize with the joy and pain of others. They generally struggle honestly with the issues of freedom and independence. Sometimes they want to assert themselves, but other times they feel vulnerable and want to be left alone. They genuinely care about their own futures and worry about such larger issues as poverty, hunger, and world peace.

While young people may give confusing signals to their parents, they look to parents for affirmation, trust, and challenge. They are encouraged by sincere praise for their accomplishments, such as tutoring a young child or trying their best in school. It is important that the lines of communication remain open even if they are sometimes strained. A parent and a young adolescent should talk about

the cultural and age differences between them and recognize those differences as opportunities to learn from one another and perhaps understand one another better. "In the face of the so-called culture of death, the family is the heart of the culture of life" (*Encyclical on the 100th Anniversary of "Rerum Novarum,"* 39).

LETTING GO WHILE BEING THERE

Painful as it may be, parents usually continue the process of letting go by sharing responsibility with young adolescents and encouraging their gradual independence. Parents render their children a service of critical importance by nurturing their growth.

Young people grow best when others are consistent and reasonable in what they expect of them. Parents help them by providing reasons for the limits they set and by explaining why certain activities are permitted and others are not. It is natural for young adolescents to question such reasons, but even so parents should go on working to bring about agreement on what is acceptable and unacceptable behavior and on the consequences of the unacceptable. Then young people know what to expect if they choose to defy parental or other legitimate authority.

Young adolescents are more likely to accept their parents' judgments, whether of praise or blame, when the day-in day-out parental attitude is one of consistent affirmation.

Generally they expect parents to listen to them, discuss with them, respond to them, and help them decide what is right and how to do it. A parent's indifference can create a gulf just when parent and child need to remain most attentive to each other.

PARENTS ARE PEOPLE TOO

Meanwhile, young people are scrutinizing their parents' values, judgments, and ways of doing things, and that, too, is normal. If they verbalize their questions, however, they can stir up unresolved issues for a parent.

But even though parents must allow for the possibility that their own ideas or actions are wrong, they nevertheless can usually trust their instincts and experiences to provide sound direction. Not every question young people ask can be answered simply or to their satisfaction, but discussion with a parent usually helps the young adolescent confront his or her feelings. The fact that a child does not fully understand the correctness of a parent's position now does not mean he or she will not understand it later.

A wholesome family life can foster interior dispositions that are a genuine preparation for a living faith and remain a support for it throughout one's life.

Catechism of the Catholic Church, 2225

In such exchanges the parent, too, is being challenged to grow. Both the parent and the young adolescent must allow each other to make mistakes without fear of harsh judgment. Obviously, though, this does not extend to dangerous mistakes like getting involved with drugs or alcohol or engaging in premarital sex. On matters like these, parents need to be more assertive and take a stronger stand. There are times when a parent must be firm and uncompromising.

Young adolescents most need parental love in difficult times and when they are hardest to love. They feel alone and isolated if they sense that a parent has given up on them.

Parents have a right to be respected, trusted, and affirmed by all who assist them in the education and formation of their children. Their participation in support groups and youth-centered activities often helps them realize what good parents they really are.

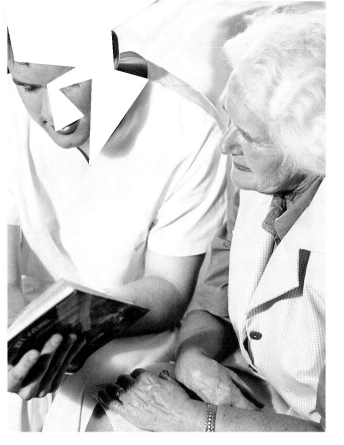

LIVING, ACTIVE, AND CONSCIOUS FAITH

The life of faith is best shared with young adolescents through experiences which provide opportunities to relate life to Christian values. Young people learn more about charity, for example, by contributing to the support of an orphan or by reading a book to a blind person than from lectures about it.

However, because young adolescents can understand the concepts or doctrines of faith, they also learn from formal catechesis. Parents and others may fully and clearly communicate the faith to adolescents by imparting knowledge of the Catholic faith, inspiring trust in God who revealed it, and urging behavior in accord with it. "A wholesome family life can foster interior dispositions that are a genuine preparation for a living faith and remain a support for it throughout one's life" (*Catechism*, 2225). The deposit of faith is the rightful heritage of young believers. They should not be deprived of it.

Parents, teachers, catechists, and youth ministers support young adolescents most effectively when they communicate regularly and cooperate with one another. Parents have much to offer catechetical programs. For example, their counsel in selecting among approved material for education in human sexuality and in planning activities and projects with and for their children can be very helpful.

THE POWER OF PEERS

While parents remain strong influences for young adolescents, peers are very significant as well. Good peer relationships are essential for healthy development, and young adolescents usually establish peer groups whose members are intensely loyal to one another. Frequently they will turn to their peers to test their feelings on matters like family difficulties, grades, popularity, and looks.

Young adolescents are seldom loners by choice. They are greatly preoccupied with the questions "What group do I belong to?" and "What group do I *want* to belong to?" They can be easily manipulated by fads, especially in music and clothes, because the expectations of others mean so much to them. They usually want to be like their peers in behavior, dress, likes and dislikes, hair styles, and language.

A parent needs to be alert for signs indicating that a young adolescent may be involved in gang activity. Strange hand gestures, bazaar dress or hair cuts, insignias, and code words can all signal a young adolescent's association with a group having a negative influence. Parents should monitor erratic behavior, disrupted sleeping habits, wide emotional

swings, or sudden physical deterioration as early warning signs of alcohol or drug dependency. Parents also need to be vigilant for signs of despair in their children. At times life can seem overwhelming for young people and death holds a peculiar attraction for them.

OTHER ROLE MODELS

Young adolescents need positive role models, mentors, heroes, and heroines. They may find them in godparents, grandparents, aunts, uncles, cousins, family friends, teachers, coaches, clergy or religious, public figures, movie stars, sports figures, television celebrities or entertainers.

These individuals can give genuine inspiration to young people and frequently support what parents are trying to develop. But they can also be negative influences. A parent should help the young adolescent distinguish between adults who are truly worthy of emulation and those who are not.

ENTHUSIASM OR INDIFFERENCE

Their emerging sense of responsibility can be a source of justifiable pride for these young people. They generally enjoy carrying out projects, sharing group experiences, role playing, and simply participating in discussions in which they can probe their values, but they need guidance in their discernment of values.

Parents need to communicate Christian values to their children and to instruct them in the teachings and tradition of the Church, for this is the proper framework in which to discern what is true and good. Children need to hear from their parents that Christian values lead people to think, judge, and act in a certain way, a Christian way. They like to become involved with social justice issues and readily join groups on hunger walks, food drives, fund-raising projects for the poor, peace marches, or resource exchanges between parishes with differing racial compositions. Such involvements are even more valuable when they can reflect on them with parents or other adults.

Sometimes, though, young adolescents can appear quite apathetic. They may even seem to shun involvement, especially in service projects or other activities that they perceive as boring or "not with it." Even so, the invitation to participate should be extended and they should still be encouraged to take part.

Parents should be aware that a young person's apathy may be his or her way of trying to communicate about a problem or a need unrecognized up to now.

Parents should seek young adolescents' opinions and listen carefully. They should also try to involve these young people in family discussions, planning, and problem solving. Time for reflection, self-discovery, and dialogue with a parent is essential for the young adolescent. This period marks the beginning of a search for meaning that will last a lifetime.

PRAYER LIFE

By the time children reach early adolescence, daily prayer continues to be an ordinary part of family life. A parent's attitude toward prayer has largely shaped the young adolescent's own feelings about prayer. If parents recognize the sacredness of all creation, pray with their children regularly, and help them identify the events of their lives as experiences of God, then the young adolescents are more likely to be comfortable with prayer as a habit of their lives.

STARTING POINTS FOR PRAYER

A family's ethnic and cultural heritage offers many opportunities for special prayerful celebrations at home. The birthday of Martin Luther King, Jr., the feast of Our Lady of Guadalupe, the feast of St. Patrick, and many other occasions hold important places in some families.

While young adolescents may feel self-conscious about making up prayers and adding them to the family's prayer, they can usually write their own prayers and share them. The psalms and other passages from Scripture are good points of departure for them. Time for personal reflection, sharing within the family, listening to music, or simply being silent encourages young people to develop a personal prayer life.

THE STRUGGLE TO PRAY

There are times when a young adolescent does not want to be present for family prayer, for everyone needs

to be alone sometimes. "...the living and true God tirelessly calls each person to that mysterious encounter known as prayer" (*Catechism*, 2567). The family should still gather for prayer at the regular time and place, even if several family members cannot be present. Forcing a young adolescent to attend family prayer causes tension where ease and freedom should be expected.

> ...the living and true God tirelessly calls each person to that mysterious encounter known as prayer.
>
> *Catechism of the Catholic Church, 2567*

Often family members will have to struggle to carve out time for family activities, such as simply being together, visiting relatives, going on an outing, or sharing a special meal. Activities that conflict with family interests should be carefully considered and evaluated.

Priorities have to be established. Family prayer grows from family life, so family members will have to make personal sacrifices to be together regularly and for significant amounts of time.

Some families designate one evening per week as "Family Night." Family members agree to keep this night free from other involvements so that they can be together. Such a block of time for family meetings, prayer, games, or other activities helps prevent fragmentation of the family and encourages closeness.

PRAYER IN THE CATHOLIC TRADITION

Regarding more formal prayer, traditional devotions such as the Rosary and the Stations of the Cross can be explained more fully to young adolescents. Praying and exploring the meaning of prayers such as the Our Father, the Apostles' Creed, the Hail Mary, and the Glory to the Father reinforces the previous learning and deepens the meaning of these prayers for the youngsters.

DO I HAVE TO GO?

In our tradition, the Lord's Day (Sunday) is a gift of God that encourages us to rest from the cares of the week and restore ourselves. Sunday's family prayer blesses the family time of renewal and leads the family to the Eucharist. Those who occupy positions of influence in young people's lives should never be ambiguous in word or example about the obligation to participate in the Sunday Eucharist; but besides pointing out the obligation, they should make clear the importance of the Eucharist to the individual and to the community of faith.

Young people often see Mass as a monotonous exercise, but they can learn that the Eucharist draws the worshiping community together and leads it towards a more faithful relationship with God. They can also learn that the community celebration of the Eucharist flows from one's own need to express faith with others. Young adolescents need to be invited to assume responsibilities within the faith community and reminded that the community worships together on Sunday, the day of the Lord's resurrection.

In early adolescence young people often begin to ask why they have to go to Mass, why the Eucharist is the same every Sunday, and why it is always so boring. A parent should respect the youngster's feelings, be patient with the grumbling, and set a good example. Perhaps exploring with the young person what we bring to the Eucharist—our hopes, our hurts, and so on—can help to demonstrate part of our motivation for worshiping together. This is a good opportunity to tell the youngster that it is normal to question the value of going to Mass, while pointing out that the questions have answers. Perhaps the parent will want to add that, although convinced of the value of Mass, he or she sometimes has the same feelings.

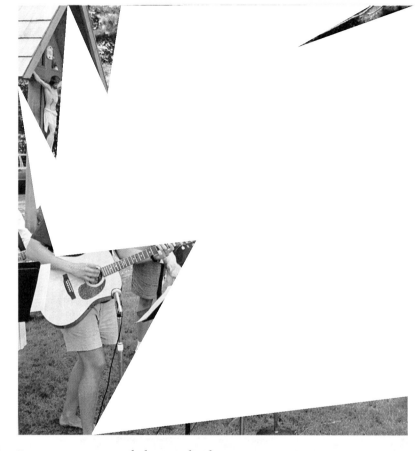

Because young people have individual relationships with God, they need opportunities to express their faith in their own ways during the celebration of the Eucharist. Masses planned by young people and for small groups of young people with the assistance of adults can help both children and adults integrate the meaning of the Eucharist in their daily lives.

In view of their profound influence on their children, parents need to be aware of their own attitudes about Sunday Mass. The day on which we remember the Lord's resurrection is different from every other day of the week. It is the day on which the faith community gathers around the table of the Lord to celebrate his memory, to share both word and sacrament, to confess its common faith, and to commit itself to a more active, living and conscious faith. In the long run, parents' personal attitudes toward Sunday Mass and the example of their lives have a far greater influence on young adolescents than parental orders to attend.

RENEWAL AND RETREAT

Young adolescents benefit greatly from days of renewal and intensive retreats. Community-building activities allow them to become involved in small groups, listen to others' opinions, and examine their own values.

To experience an extended, prayerful time with people their own age can be an especially powerful and rewarding experience for young adolescents. Opportunities for group as well as private prayer, and sung as well as silent prayer, help young people value prayer and grow in their love for God. Family knowledge of, and some involvement in a day of renewal or retreat is essential and can be another measure of support for when the young person returns home.

CHURCH LIFE

As they work at establishing a framework for their benefits, attitudes, and values, young adolescents will—one hopes—look to the faith community for direction. They want to belong, to participate in the faith life of the community, and to be of service to it. In small group gatherings and with competent guidance, for example, they can become enthusiastic about learning how to listen to their peers' hopes and fears and to respond with care.

The Spirit will teach us everything, remind us of all that Christ said to us and bear witness to him.

Catechism of the Catholic Church, 729

INVOLVEMENT IN PARISH LIFE

If young adolescents feel at home in the parish, they are more apt to look there for support when they need it. They can also be energetic resources for the parish community. When asked to help with hospitality at parish events, serve as ushers, work on parish fund-raising projects, visit the sick and elderly, care for younger children, or be aides in various programs, they usually respond generously and welcome direction from adults. They have a genuine hunger to learn and to serve, especially if they can work with a friend or a small group. Young people should remember that "The Spirit will teach us everything, remind us of all that Christ said to us and bear witness to him" (*Catechism*, 729).

Obviously, children need to receive the sacraments but their sacramental participation is enriched when parents and teachers are successful in involving them more broadly in the sacramental life of the parish. They may enjoy writing notes to parents whose infants are being baptized.

Besides parish school and catechetical programs for young adolescents, programs for their parents can also be very helpful. Workshops on parenting, communication, alcohol and substance abuse can help them deal with perplexing questions. Often the most effective programs bring parents and young people together to discuss mutual concerns.

Communication in religious matters between a parent and a young adolescent is especially important. The explicit sharing of religious beliefs, values, and practice can be difficult for parents, but it makes a lasting impression on their children. When parents speak of their own faith, of how they came to believe, of the doubts they had over the years, and of why they continue to believe, young adolescents usually listen carefully.

LEARNING OBJECTIVES FOR YOUNG ADOLESCENTS

In formal catechetical programs, junior high students learn that love and service are essential elements in the covenant relationship that God has established with us. They learn about the history of the Church, about its mission, and about ministry in the Church. They learn about the structure and governance of the

They might like to "adopt" a first communicant. They can plan a party for the children who have celebrated the sacrament of Reconciliation for the first time. They can choose service projects as a part of their own preparation for the sacrament of Confirmation. They can be "welcomers" or "name tag makers" at a communal celebration of the sacrament of the Anointing of the Sick.

Young adolescents also need simply to have fun at the parish. Parties, athletic events, informal drop-ins, and junior high clubs help them enjoy parish life. They do not want to be perceived as strangers or spectators waiting to get older in order to be taken seriously.

Church and the specific gifts that the various ministries—pope, bishop, pastors, lay ministers—offer the Church. They learn that the Church is a complex reality: the Body of Christ, a pilgrim people, a sign of Christ's love, and an institution. They become acquainted with the gospel portraits of Jesus as proclaimer of the kingdom, Savior of all, liberator of the oppressed, and the way to the Father. They begin to study the Old Testament more deeply. They learn about the gift of God's grace in the sacraments of initiation as well as the sacraments of healing and commitment. They learn that Mary is Mother of the Church and a perfect model of obedience, humility, and faith for all to imitate. In addition, junior high students learn that Mary, because of her role in salvation history as the Mother of God, was preserved from sin from the first moment of her own life and was assumed into heaven after her death.

YOUNG ADOLESCENT MORALITY

Internalization of Christian values, conscience formation, decision making, and accountability are important parts of young adolescents' religious formation. A sense of personal responsibility for behavior and the ability to integrate specific Christian principles of conduct begin to emerge.

Young people learn that personal conscience involves a fundamental set of Christian values and an obligation to live by them, as well as the judgment that a person makes about the goodness or evil of a specific action. Help in forming one's conscience comes from the experience of living in a Christian home, Scripture, the teachings of the Church, personal prayer, study and reflection, as well as the example of Jesus and the saints. Young adolescents learn that basic moral truths, for example, those rooted in the sanctity of human life, do not change and are not to be violated in any situation.

THE SACRAMENT OF CONFIRMATION

Junior high students are normally invited to prepare for the sacrament of Confirmation. A parent should help the young adolescent consider significant questions of faith, such as *"What does it mean to be a Catholic?"* and *"How important is the Catholic faith to me?"*

While the age for Confirmation may vary, preparation for it should be appropriate to the age of those being confirmed, should involve parents, sponsors, and the parish community, and should include elements of community service and the presence of trained adult advisors. A young person's readiness for Confirmation depends on the ability to give witness to the faith. While Confirmation is ordinarily celebrated in the junior high years—that is, between the ages of 12 and 14—a lot more is involved in the decision for Confirmation than age, grade, or social pressure. The close collaboration of the young adolescent, the parent, and the pastoral staff helps determine both the method of preparation and the appropriate time for Confirmation. In some circumstances, it might be desirable to delay Confirmation until a young person is ready, as measured by a more mature view of faith and religious practice.

The gift of faith given in Baptism is strengthened in Confirmation and nourished in the Eucharist. In some dioceses, in fact, the preferred order for reception of these sacraments is: Baptism, Confirmation, Eucharist. This manner of celebration is rooted historically in the early Church. However, over the centuries, and for a variety of reasons, the order for celebrating these sacraments underwent change. Many, perhaps most, Catholics today receive Confirmation some time after their first sharing of the Eucharist. Regardless of the order of reception, a parent's focus needs to remain on the spiritual growth of the young person, and the call of God to live together as a family of Christian discipleship.

As the primary educators of their children, parents can make significant contributions to a program of preparation for Confirmation.

Their involvement strengthens their own faith and gives them another opportunity to set a good example for their young adolescents. A parent can offer much encouragement to the youthful idealism of an adolescent.

Confirmation renews and strengthens the Christian's baptismal call to bear witness to Christ in the world. It emphasizes the transformation of the person's life in Christ by the outpouring of the Holy Spirit. The person being confirmed is empowered by the Spirit to share a living, conscious, and active faith with others. The presence of the congregation at the celebration of this sacrament signifies that the whole Christian community offers—and owes—its continued support and concern to the personal, maturing commitment made when a young person is anointed and sealed with the gift of the Holy Spirit.

Receiving the sacrament of Confirmation marks not the end of young adolescents' religious development but the beginning of another stage. As confirmed Christians, young people are challenged to share their faith with others. Service in the Church and in society—government, business, education, science, labor, and many other fields—will provide them with opportunities to work for justice and charity, human dignity and rights, in a variety of occupations. Learning this, they also learn that Christian values such as mercy, peace, compassion, and forgiveness should lead them in their everyday judgments and decisions.

Parents should welcome and respect with joy and thanksgiving the Lord's call to one of their children to follow him in virginity for the sake of the Kingdom in the consecrated life or in priestly ministry.

Catechism of the Catholic Church, 2233

VOCATIONS AND CAREER CHOICES

Committed Christians respond to this challenge in various vocations or states of life. Marriage, the single life, the ordained priesthood, the permanent diaconate, religious life—these are all vocational commitments that in turn lend themselves to a multitude of different ministries and apostolates. "Parents should welcome and respect with joy and thanksgiving the Lord's call to one of their children to follow him in virginity for the sake of the Kingdom in the consecrated life or in priestly ministry" (*Catechism*, 2233).

Young adolescents naturally spend a good deal of time visualizing their possible futures and considering their careers. Now is the time for parents to help them think more seriously about vocation and life choices. So, for example, a parent can discuss with the adolescent the permanent, faithful, and creative love celebrated in Christian marriage. However, "Parents should be careful not to exert pressure on their children either in the choice of a profession or in that of a spouse" (*Catechism*, 2230).

Days of recollection or retreats on the theme of vocations can help young people focus their questions and feelings about what they want to do with their lives.

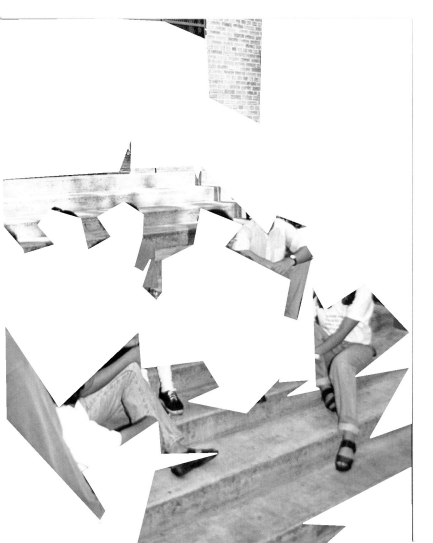

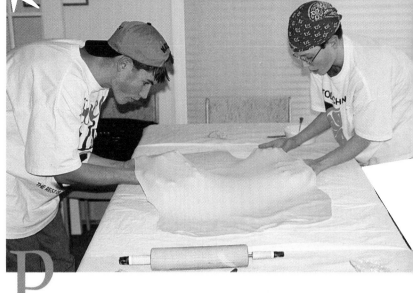

BEYOND CONFIRMATION

Formal catechetical and formation programs for young people are most effective within a total youth ministry that includes instruction, community building, opportunities for service, and liturgical celebrations. The social, recreational, and spiritual activities of young people can take various forms, and the planning can involve parents, other adults with special abilities in youth ministry, and the young people themselves. The active involvement of parents who visit classes, participate in projects, and offer help in support of the catechetical objectives adds a unique and valuable dimension to youth ministry.

Parents should be careful not to exert pressure on their children either in the choice of a profession or in that of a spouse.

Catechism of the Catholic Church, 2230

A parent should make it a particular point to encourage his or her child to consider a vocation to the priesthood or religious life. Throughout a child's religious development, parents need to provide opportunities for their children to get to know priests and women and men religious as people, not just as functionaries. A parent's own attitude toward priests and religious strongly influences the young person's attitude. If young adolescents are going to be attracted to the priesthood or religious life, it is important that they sense a deep respect for priests and religious in their own parents.

Reflection QUESTIONS

1. *What do I see in my own child that reminds me of my own adolescence?*

2. *What can I offer my child that was not available when I was a child?*
   What can the Church offer? What can society offer?

3. *What is most lovable about my child?*

4. *How do I share my doubts and uncertainties with my child?*

5. *What is my deepest hope for my child's future?*

Quotations from Church
D O C U M E N T S

The gospel of love is the inexhaustible source of all that nourishes the human family as a communion of persons. In love the whole educational process finds its support and definitive meaning as the mature fruit of the parents' mutual gift. Through the efforts, sufferings and disappointments which are part of every person's education, love is constantly being put to the test.

Pope John Paul II,
Letter to Families, 16

As the primary educators of their children, parents, along with sponsors, are to be intimately involved in catechesis for Confirmation. This will help them renew and strengthen their own faith, besides enabling them to set a better example for their children or godchildren.

National Catechetical
Directory, 119

The home is well suited for *education in the virtues*. This requires an apprenticeship in self-denial, sound judgment, and self-mastery—the preconditions of all true freedom.

Catechism of the Catholic Church, 2223

Catechesis for justice, mercy and peace is a continuing process which concerns every person and every age. It first occurs in the family by word and example.

National Catechetical Directory, 170

The tragic fate of too many children is not simply an economic or social problem, but a sign of moral failure and a religious test.

Putting Children and Families First